FROGLOGIC

FIELD MANUALS FOR ADULTS

Self-Confidence

by

David Rutherford

NAVY SEAL

&

BEHAVIORAL TRAINING SPECIALIST

Froglogic Concepts, LLC
2101 NW Corporate Boulevard, Suite 206
Boca Raton, FL 33431

Leadline Publishing titles may be purchased for business or promotional use or for special sales. For information please contact our editor in chief, Charles Rutherford, Leadline Publishing, at cer@teamfroglogic.com

First Leadline paperback published in 2007.

Library of Congress Cataloging-in-Publication Data

Rutherford, David B.

Froglogic, Field Manuals for Adults, vol.1 'Self-Confidence' / David B. Rutherford

p. cm.

Includes glossary.

ISBN – 978 – 0 – 9801464 – 3 - 1

1. Education   2. Self-Help techniques

First Edition Copyright © 2012

About the Author

David Rutherford is a Navy SEAL and Behavioral Training Specialist. During his time in the SEAL Teams he was a student, combat paramedic, operator and instructor. He participated in clandestine operations in the Middle East, South Asia and Southeast Asia. After leaving his career in the SEALs, he has worked extensively overseas as an international training and security specialist for one of the largest defense contractors in the world and for the US Government. David created the Froglogic Concept in April of 2006. Since then, he has exposed countless numbers of kids and adults around the world to his elite lifestyle performance program. He believes anyone can attain their dreams by forging their Self-Confidence and committing themselves to living the Team Life. David spreads his unique, high energy message around the globe as a motivational speaker, author, life instructor and TV personality. For more information on David Rutherford, please visit his website at www.teamfroglogic.com.

Disclaimer

The expressed written opinions in this book are based solely on the experiences and teachings of David Rutherford. If you have any pre-existing health conditions, physical or mental, you should consult with your doctor prior to doing any of the exercises or evolutions listed in this book. Do not attempt any of the US Navy SEAL BUDS style training evolutions. These activities are extremely dangerous and could result in serious injury or death. This book is designed to help motivate and inspire adults to start using Froglogic as a way of developing a healthy lifestyle by forging their *Self-Confidence* and living the *Team Life*. HOOYAH.

Froglogic Definition:

Froglogic (frog-lojik), n. 1. A way of thinking that perpetually activates an individual's desire to forge his or her own *Self-Confidence* in order to commit to living a team orientated lifestyle or *Team Life*. 2. A two-part motivational training program. Part 1. Accepting 8 Life Missions into your lifestyle in order to forge your personal and professional Self-Confidence. Part 2. Committing to 4 simple Missions that will ignite your understanding of what it means to live the Team Life. 3. A concept rooted in the proven experiences of over 70 years of UDT/ SEAL Real World operations, training doctrine and elite lifestyle performance.

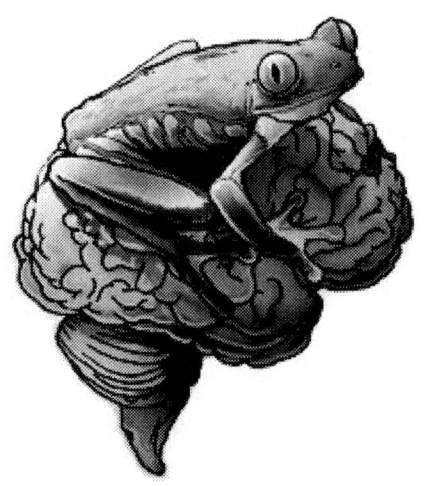

Forward

"Greater love hath no man than this, that a man lay down his life for his friends." No other man I know can fit this quote as perfectly as Dave. David Rutherford, Navy SEAL, Motivational Speaker, Author and Life Instructor, has put his life on the line for his teammates on the battlefield and his teammates in the civilian world. Due to this love for his fellow brethren, I have had the privilege to become one of his teammates. David and I found each other while we were on a missionary trip in Haiti back in the summer of 2009. At that time, I was experiencing serious conflict, internally and externally. I wanted to achieve something huge in my life. I wanted to make something of myself. However, I was too wrapped up in partying to go after my dream. What held me back the most was fear. I was afraid of what would happen if I abandoned this chaotic, unmotivated lifestyle and went with my gut feeling to achieve something greater. David helped me look past this fear. He showed me what really mattered in life, and he taught me how to get there. I started working with Dave not long after our missionary trip. Since the first day we started training, he's been hammering the Froglogic Concepts into me. During our time together he showed me the vitality of commitment, training, communication and leadership in living the Team Life. He also taught me how to improve my Self-Confidence by maintaining a positive attitude, setting goals and living with integrity. Now I'm always striving to forge my development, and most importantly, making sure I'm having fun in the process. With these Froglogic Concepts, among many others, I've come a long way from the chaotic lifestyle of my past. I'm now a cadet at VMI and hope one day to become a true Warrior Poet. I still have a long way to go to accomplish my mission, but I know with the help of my team and the ideals ingrained in my being through Froglogic, I will get there. Froglogic works; I am a testament to that. Don't take my word for it though. Drive on through this book and unlock the pearls that it holds, and as Dave would say, "GET FIRED UP!"

Froglogic Teammate

For Blair

The Fire in my Gut

FROGLOGIC
FIELD MANUALS FOR ADULTS

Self-Confidence
8 Life Missions To Forge Your Self-Confidence

Intro

The Froglogic Concept is a way of thinking that will radically change your lifestyle and prepare you to feel and achieve mission success every day. Over the past twenty years I have been on a journey of discovery to find where the true nature of a *human being's* successes and failures come from. My journey has taken me around the world as a student, a Navy SEAL, an international training specialist, a motivational speaker, author and coach for kids and adults. Throughout my travels, I have felt and I have seen people in every known emotional and cognitive state. I have seen and met people from all walks of life and challenged them to perform in the most austere physical and mental environments imaginable. I have tested the *Froglogic Concept* on humans aged 5 to 75, and inevitably the results are always the same. Using Froglogic will help you succeed. Period!

Human Being – *A person who possesses and uses empathetic logic and focused behavior to guide life's journey.*

The truth behind my discovery lies within my own forging process as well as the 70 plus years of Underwater Demolition Teams (UDT) and US Navy SEAL Teams (SEAL) development, training, operations and elite lifestyle performance. The *Brotherhood*, as we are known amongst each other, has sacrificed and bled in every American war, conflict and fight since WWII. Our effort has taken a dramatic toll on the lives of our families, friends and Teammates. However, it was not and is not in vain. The SEAL Teams are now considered one of the best special operations units in the world. It is because of our Self-Confidence and commitment to each other and our country that we achieve total mission success in the ominous face of an ever-present danger against our way of life. We will never quit.

The Brotherhood – A name used by Navy SEALs to describe the loyalty, honor and commitment we show one another in work and in life.

Now, after years of requests, I have finally written the first in a series of *Field Manuals for Adults* I call 'Froglogic - Self-Confidence.' Froglogic Field Manuals for Adults will act as instructional manuals to use in redefining and forging your new life. Discover the truths behind your ability to succeed. Your success lies in your ability to understand and face head-on the ominous challenges of life. Life requires a steel-like Self-Confidence to endure and never accept defeat. Begin your transformation and start forging your *Self-Confidence* by accepting 8 simple missions that will change your life forever.

When you embed Froglogic into your emotional and

cognitive existence and commit your life to achieving the core missions, physically, mentally and spiritually, success is inevitable. There are two main ideas that encompass the *Froglogic Concept*: (1) Self-Confidence is everything; (2) Nobody achieves alone. Once you develop *real world Self-Confidence* and adjust your way of thinking toward living a *Team Life*, you've got it. Easy day.

Froglogic Concept – (1) Self-Confidence is everything. (2) Nobody achieves alone.

Froglogic Self-Confidence – The internal perpetual drive to acknowledge, face and overcome the intense fragility of life as a Warrior Poet.

Froglogic Team Life – A Warrior Poet's ultimate commitment to living a team oriented life.

Froglogic Field Manuals for Adults – Instructional manuals to use in redefining and forging your new life.

My journey towards discovering these truths began when I lost my *Self-Confidence* and commitment to living a *Team Life* in college. I fell into an abyss of depression and self-doubt because I allowed my fear of failure to temporarily destroy my drive to realize my childhood dream. When I was growing up I always dreamed of being something bigger than life. Like many kids I wanted to play Football at the division one level and win the Heisman trophy. Fortunately my childhood dream did not come true. If it had, I wouldn't be writing you now. I spent four years adrift trying to recover from the realization that my entire existence was based on the materialization of something that simply wasn't going to happen the way I had dreamed it would. My Self-Confidence was smashed and instead of salvaging my dream, I allowed what I saw as failure to smother my motivation with negativity and a lack of self-worth. It didn't take very long to lose my direction in life. I hid behind a false persona fueled by party after party and destructive behavior. Eventually I was failing out of school, kicked off the varsity lacrosse team, and I isolated myself from the friends who were trying to help me.

Thankfully in April of 1995 I had the first epiphany of my life. One Sunday I sat in a small laundromat just off campus and watched my laundry spin in the machine. Round and round it went. Watching the laundry made me feel like I too was spiraling out of control and soaked with fear. I felt like I had no purpose in life. I was alone, lost and afraid. Miraculously, in an instant, I was awakened by something inside my soul telling me it was time to change course and begin down a new path. It was like a fire ignited in my gut. I believe this fire is in all of us, you just have to want to feel it. In that moment I felt the burn. After examining my options it was apparent that I needed to reignite the very concepts that defined my successes as a child. As a kid I was filled with Self-Confidence because of what I learned being on a team. The critical lessons I learned about pushing yourself for the betterment of the team were the cornerstones of my success both on and off the field. It was time to regain my *Self-Confidence* and become a part of a team. The concept is so simple and clear. In that moment I decided to become a member of one of the most elite teams on the planet, the SEAL Teams.

Within months of my epiphany, I was being exposed to a proven mindset that would ultimately shape my success for the rest of my life. The forging process of my *Self-Confidence* and commitment to a *Team Life* was not easy. My experiences in the SEAL Teams as a student, operator, medic and instructor were incredibly difficult. A real breakthrough of discovery came during my tenure as an SQT (SEAL Qualification Training) Instructor. Because of manning needs within our community, I was taken out of my second platoon at SEAL Team One and reassigned to the Naval Special Warfare Center as an SQT Medical instructor. Unfortunately for me, a SEAL's expertise is measured by the amount of *platoon deployments* an operator has experienced. At this point in my career I had only completed one platoon work up and deployment. My arrival at SQT as a "one platoon wonder" was concerning to me. I doubted myself and my ability to have a meaningful impact on the students.

Fortunately, with the help of a few incredible teammates and mentors, especially my Senior Chief, I was able to discover one of my greatest strengths as an instructor and human being, my passion for motivating.

Platoon – A 16 man squad of SEALs who carry out clandestine missions around the world.

Deployment – A 6-month period when SEALs are overseas conducting clandestine operations around the world.

During my time at SQT I discovered that in order for a human being to comprehensively learn a metric ton of complicated information in a microscopic period of time and accomplish *Mission Success* in the most extreme physical and mental environments known to humanity, he or she must first be motivated to embrace a higher level of commitment. The inspired ability to succeed is directly attributable to a human's individual Self-Confidence as it relates to their commitment to the team around them. These core concepts are the proven concepts responsible for the incredible historical successes of the Underwater Demolition Teams and the SEAL Teams. They are also the concepts I learned going through *BUDS, 18 Delta, SQT* and my first and second platoons at SEAL Team One. I became the Instructor responsible for instilling the very same motivational concepts that helped forge me. With my discovery, the Froglogic Concept was born.

BUDS – *Basic Underwater Demolition SEAL School: A grueling 24 week course that acts as the gateway to the SEAL Teams.*

SQT – *SEAL Qualification Training Program: An exhausting 26 week finishing school that certifies BUDS graduates are ready to join a SEAL Team and grants them the distinguished honor of wearing the Navy SEAL insignia, the SEAL Trident.*

18.Delta – *Joint Special Operations Combat Medic Training Short Course – A 24 week academic hammer session ending with real world patient contact in major trauma areas in the US.*

SEAL Platoon Work up and Deployment – *18 months of high-speed special operations training followed by a 6 month deployment overseas.*

Since leaving the Navy in 2003, I have continued my journey as both student and instructor, proving the value of applying Froglogic in my life. In 2006 I had another epiphany, another awakening in my soul that lit the fire in my gut, a fire that has fueled my purpose in life ever since. At the time, I was traveling the world as an international training specialist, training foreign commandos on how to operate at higher levels of proficiency. Over the course of my travels, both in and out of the military, I have been emotionally *hammered* by the incomprehensible conditions children are facing around the globe, especially in countries run by corrupt dictatorial regimes. This reality altered my path, opened my heart and forged a new direction in my life. In April of that year, I accepted a new *Life Mission* and hung up my bulletproof vest for the moment and devoted myself to writing my first *Field Manual for Kids*.

Life Mission – A person's purpose or objective that is driven by the perpetual desire to develop his or her physical, mental and spiritual self for the greater good.

Fire in the Gut – A SEAL motto that describes the insatiable desire to be better, to push yourself harder and to achieve mission success no matter what the cost.

My purpose, my calling, my Life Mission is to expose kids and adults to the benefits of using Froglogic in their lives. My Life Mission is to help people around the globe, but especially in America, realize just how simple it is to achieve success through the forging of *Self-Confidence* and living a committed *Team Life*. For the past 6 years I have shared Froglogic with hundreds of thousands around the world. Now with this new *Field Manual for Adults* I am going to expose millions more to the Froglogic Concept. HOOYAH!

Your Teammate,
David Rutherford

TEAM FROGLOGIC

WARNING ORDER

Team Froglogic Warning Order #001 - #008

Issued by motivational instructor/ D. Rutherford aka "RUT"

Time/Date – ACTION REQUIRED IMMEDIATELY

Situation:

Life has been challenging. You have lost a bit of the fire in your gut and need help getting it back. You have recognized that you can't do it alone and have decided to recruit Team Froglogic to help get you Squared Away.

Mission Tasking:

Your *Mission tasking* is to forge your *Self-Confidence* by applying the 8 missions laid out in this Froglogic Field Manual for Adults.

General Instructions:

A. Special Teams/ Task Organization

Your team consists of all those who love you and want to help you. Utilize them every day to achieve total mission success.

B. Uniform and Equipment Common to All

The uniform of the day is whatever makes you feel part of the team. Your special equipment is any and all necessary equipment to help you with your mission tasking.

C. Special Equipment

Your special equipment should be at least one little item that constantly reminds you to work on your *Self-Confidence*. Example: a rock, a pendent, a bracelet, a photo, a song, your swim buddy, or this field manual. Something or someone that is always there in your life.

D. Tentative Time Schedule

24 hours a day. 7 days a week. 365 days a year.

Special Instructions:

All italicized words are keywords to know and are defined in the glossary.

The only easy day was yesterday!

PT Instructions

The PT Schedule listed in the front of each Mission is designed to get your body and mind right before you begin reading. There is nothing better than working out the built-up energy and stress in your body prior to using your mind. Conducting at least 30 minutes of vigorous exercise every day will begin getting you dialed in to forge your *Self-Confidence*. Rest when you need to rest. I realize that you might be reading this field manual on a plane or on a business trip; no sweat. Each PT consists of exercises that you can conduct in a 6' x 4' area that I call *The Box*. The Box is an imaginary space in your office, hotel or living room floor where you can effectively perform each exercise perfectly. So, GET IN THE BOX!

5 minute stretch

Jumping Jacks

Half Jacks

Air Squats

Stationary Lunges

Regular Pushups

Wide Pushups

Diamond Pushups

Sit-ups

Leg Levers

Crunches

Extended Leg Crunches

Side Crunches

4 Count Flutter Kicks

8 Count Body Builders

Visit my website at www.teamfroglogic.com for instructions and videos on how to perform each exercise.

Mission 1: Have a Positive Attitude

Mission 1: Have a Positive Attitude

Operational Objectives:

∞ *Use the following steps to support the hardening of your positive attitude as it relates to forging your Self-Confidence.* ∞

Step 1 - Anchor Your Heart to Your Mind

Step 2 - Start Everyday Cold, Wet and Sandy

Step 3 - Find a Swim Buddy

Step 4 - No Whining

Question: Are you more often a negative or positive person?

∞ *Think about this question as you read this Mission and relate your life to ideas presented.* ∞

PT Schedule:

5 minute stretch

25 - Jumping Jacks

25 - Half Jacks

50 - Air Squats

25 - Regular Pushups

15 - Wide Pushups

10 - Diamond Pushups

25 - Sit-ups

25 - Leg Levers

25 - Crunches

25 - 4 Count Flutter Kicks

10 - 8 Count Body Builders

Have a positive attitude. WOW, is it really that simple? YES! While you read this field manual, I want you to remember that this is not Rocket Science. We are simply forging the most basic part of the human condition needed to have *Self-Confidence*. Why do I use the term forging? Because it's tough, right? Wrong! It's because I want to create a mental image in your mind that is simple for you to associate with your physical, mental and spiritual development. With forging we immediately envision some soot-covered blacksmith from the 12th century hammering away at a piece of raw steel, sparks exploding off a giant broad sword as this massive man smites his hammer against his anvil. I'll admit this image is pretty tough and the idea of smashing yourself in any way is a little dramatic, but that's what it takes to change something inside yourself. That's what it takes to forge your *Self-Confidence:* the power and intestinal fortitude to hammer away at the raw material within you. Your internal strength is what forges your greatest weapon, the steel within your soul that is your *Self-Confidence*.

Every day we are under assault by the constant barrage of negativity *sniping* away at our psyche. We are facing new challenges that our world has never imagined or experienced before. According to the UN, 9 billion people will be on the planet by

2050. Think about that. Think about what role you are going the play in this explosion of change. How are you going to make an impact? Whatever course you chart, you will need *Self-Confidence* to cut the right path in a life that has so many elements colliding with each other.

Why is having *Self-Confidence* so important in our lives? Because *Self-Confidence* is everything. It is the foundation of your positive or negative existence. With it you take risk, face adversity, accept failure and embrace your fears. YOU SUCCEED! Without it you are held captive by your fear of the unknown. Once you develop *Real World Self-Confidence* and adjust your way of thinking towards living a *Team Life*, you've got it. Think about your average day. How many times during that day does your *Self-Confidence* play a role in the decisions you make?

Now think about the days filled with the unforeseen challenges that can cause overwhelming doubt and outright fear. Fear is the greatest enemy you will face in your life. I am talking about the types of fears that will generate hesitation and procrastination every day if you let it. Fear of asking for help. Fear of commitment. Fear of saying no. Fear of taking a risk. Fear of failure. These fears impede your ability to succeed every day of the week. If you agree, let out a loud and thunderous *HOOYAH*!

Real World – A factual life experience that isn't based on theory or conjecture. An event that actually happens and has a profound impact on your perspective.

HOOYAH – The War cry or Battle cry of the SEAL Teams. Used in a variety of ways, but mostly to express extreme passion in a particular situation.

You combat all types of fears with your *Self-Confidence*. The more self-confident you are, the easier it is to accept the never-ending struggles associated with life and embrace all the successes you deserve. In case you haven't figured it out by now, LIFE IS HARD! We all face adversity in our lives. Some people face much more than others. Think about the youth of Afghanistan who are in their 20's and 30's. These young adults have known nothing other than war. For their entire lives their country has been dominated by the hardships and atrocities of decades of conflict. The *Self-Confidence* required to endure this type of hopelessness is truly inspiring. I have been traveling back and forth to Afghanistan since 2002 and have worked with hundreds of Afghans living this reality.

Maybe you could use an example relative to your life. How many people do you know who have been effected by the recession? Who in your life is in a trench of negativity because they lost their job or their home? Perhaps you have been affected by the last ten years of war like I have? These problems feed off one another and spread negativity like a plague devouring our physical, mental and spiritual selves.

Historical Debrief

On March 4, 1933, our nation was at one of the lowest points in its history. Twenty-five percent of the nation's workforce was unemployed and over 2 million people were homeless. Banks in thirty-two states were unable to open their doors for business and the New York Federal Reserve was broke. During his 1933 inaugural address, Franklin D. Roosevelt included a statement that encompasses the greatest challenge we face as human beings. He said, "So, first of all, let me assert my firm belief that the only thing we have to fear is fear itself - nameless, unreasoning, unjustified terror which paralyzes needed efforts to convert retreat into advance." In context this statement was a call to arms for all Americans. The President was asking everyone to dig deep into their hearts and alter their perspective. FDR was challenging the country to stop being afraid of the depression and redefine it in their minds. He was motivating people to have a Positive Attitude. I am calling on you to do that now.

Self-Confidence begins with a *positive attitude*. Are you more often a negative or positive person? I ask this question all the time at my events and the typical answer is that most people, while sitting in front of their peers, bosses and teachers say they're positive. I say Hogwash! The truth is overwhelmingly the opposite. I see it every day no matter where I am or what I'm doing. So many people around the world are locked up in a verbal jujitsu of negativity. Almost every aspect of our culture has been infiltrated with some form of negativity. It permeates from all forms of media, including TV, movies, the web and video games. Think about the last show or movie you watched. How much of the dialogue was negative or had undercurrents of negativity? Even how we interact socially has been hijacked by narcissistic sarcasm. This type of exchange is so common that even children are treating each other with indignation and disrespect while trying to mimic the influential adults in their lives. The lexicon of our society has been overtaken by a negative insurgency hell-bent on transforming our interactions into a coded world of fear-based dialogue. People are petrified to talk to one another with pure intention and from the heart. Having a positive attitude is your armor against life's negativity penetrating your soul.

BUDS STORY:

Making it through Hellweek was one of the greatest accomplishments in my life. The experience radically altered my perspective on the importance of having a positive attitude. In case you aren't familiar with the details of *Hellweek*, allow me to explain. Hellweek is a 5 day ultra-evolution in Basic Underwater Demolition SEAL training that lasts from Sunday afternoon to Friday afternoon. During this ultra-evolution trainees sleep for about 4 hours total, burn about 7000 calories a day, run *4 mile timed beach runs*, swim *2 mile timed ocean swims*, conduct *Surf Passage* in giant surf and complete timed *O'Courses*. Plus, they receive a constant hammering of mental and physical abuse from sadistic instructors in the guise of *Elephant Runs*, freezing *Steel Piers* and the infamous *Surf Torture*, to name just a few. Imagine not sleeping for 5 straight days, suffering from complete sleep deprivation, hydrophobia and hallucinations, while trying to complete the normal physical test of regular training while having to cognitively solve problems that have no real solutions from instructors who are trying to get you to quit. What makes this ultra-evolution so unimaginable is the fact that trainees have volunteered for this physical, mental and spiritual hammer session to fuel the *fire in their gut*. This seemingly insane gut-check is the ultimate gatekeeper for the SEAL community.

Hellweek – A 5 day ultra-evolution in BUDS that acts as the initial gateway for young tadpoles who want to become SEALs. This is the first real physical, mental and spiritual test a young recruit faces in his career. See glossary for evolution definitions.

Hellweek is psychologically designed to induce a combat related mindset by exposing the trainees to exceptionally high levels of physical and mental stress and fatigue without the combat. Students are asked to push themselves beyond any previously imagined *Comfort Zone Behavior* behavior and enter new psychological waters. Hellweek is one of the greatest ultra-evolutions known to all military and civilian training around the world.

Comfort Zone Behavior – *Learned emotional and cognitive behavior human beings use to create the physical, mental and spiritual boundaries in their life that protect and mitigate from feeling and thinking about logical or illogical fear.*

When I finally made it to Hellweek in class 208, I'd been at BUDS for almost seven months. I had seen my original classmates start and graduate training. Overjoyed with the reality that I had finally made it to this epic event, I remember telling myself that, no matter what, I was going to try to enjoy Hellweek. That's right, enjoy Hellweek! Or as much as any human being can enjoy being physically and mentally thrashed for 132 hours straight.

It didn't take long for the painful reality of this ultra-evolution to begin taking its toll. Within two hours of *Breakout*, our 7-man boat crew was down to 5 men. Two of the guys who I thought were as strong as any in training decided that the program wasn't for them and *rang out*. Ringing out is when a student has decided to *DOR*, or *Drop On Request*. This means he has decided to quit training. During Hellweek there is a large nautical ship bell that follows students everywhere they go and is available for quitters to ring out at any time of the day or night. *The Bell* is normally positioned outside the 1st Phase office of the main compound. Losing two guys was a real blow to the rest of us who not only lost friends but also had to suck up the slack of not having those two strong bodies underneath our boat.

We rallied by laughing at the circumstances and for the extra attention promised us by the instructors. You see, my boat crew leader was the son of the acting Admiral, who had previously visited his son during training and dutifully ordered the instructors of 1st Phase to make sure that he and his boat crew got "extra attention." Our camaraderie and ability to convert this potentially debilitating situation into a positive one by simply using laughter and maintaining a positive attitude was just what we all needed to endure the next 24 hours of training without a full boat crew of 7.

For the next 5 days we were beaten down and forced to test our intestinal fortitude. The instructors had to strip us of any previously learned cognitive or emotional limitations. It is critical to the success of the SEAL community to filter out those individuals who lack the *Self-Confidence* to endure Hellweek. Tuesday night we were put through Steel Pier twice. On Wednesday we conducted Surf Passage in 25-foot surf, the biggest surf in a decade. This beating was followed up with Surf Torture for about two hours at night. On Thursday when we felt like zombies we had to run the O' course with our boats and then at night paddled them from the shoreline in front of BUDS, around Coronado Island and back to the mud flats on the San Diego Bay side of the Silver Stand. The paddle took 14 hours. By Friday we entered the *SEAL Zone*. Our individual *Self-Confidence* was completely redefined and our commitment to each other made unbreakable. When we finally reached the infamous *Demo Pit*, our new attitudes had been forged. There was nothing we couldn't do, alone or as a team. Hellweek SECURED!

When I was secured from Hellweek I realized one of the greatest personal discoveries of my life. I truly understood that I could accomplish anything I wanted as long as I put the full force of my heart and mind behind my effort. Unbreakable *Self-Confidence* and an impenetrable *positive attitude* were the essential tools I used to finish Hellweek. This was quite a discovery because once you truly understand you have these abilities, there are no more excuses in your life.

Step 1 - Anchor your Heart to your Mind

A positive attitude is a reflection of your ability to correlate your heart's desires or dreams with your ability to think about this feeling in a rational manner. Nobody really wants to see the world as a never-ending river of hopelessness, but through years of conditioning and cultural adherence to the status quo of negativity, people allow their rational thinking to overpower their hopes and dreams. This is why humans get stuck in the ruts of life. The foundation of your positive attitude relies on your ability to look at life as a gift and an opportunity to achieve your dreams every day. Your *Self-Confidence* is never going to be forged with a negative attitude. *Self-Confidence* is built upon a positive attitude.

Are you happy with your job? Are you capable of a healthy relationship? Are you fulfilling your dreams? If you didn't answer yes to all of these very simple questions then you need to recognize that your way of thinking is *UNSAT*, or unsatisfactory! Life is short. Making the most of the incredibly brief time we are alive begins with allowing your heart and mind to work together, much like it did when you were a child. The impulsive inspiration of our youth was driven by the infinite possibility of our heart's desire. We didn't allow the reality of hard work and failure to inhibit our creative minds. If we wanted to be professional football players, we imagined we were. When my friends and I played *kill the man with the ball*, I remember running around screaming, "I'm Earl Campbell, nobody can tackle me!" I also remember sneaking around my back yard wearing my camouflage fatigues and face paint pretending to be a Special Forces soldier, shooting bottle rockets. Whatever my heart desired, I became. Allow your actions to manifest your dreams. It worked for me.

It wasn't until I allowed the fear of hard work to enter my mind that fear began impacting my cognitive understanding of achieving my dreams. In college I allowed the mere thought of facing other highly skilled football players stop me from trying to walk on at Penn State. Here I had devoted my whole life to football since I was five and didn't even give it a shot. The fear of failure overcame my heart's desire to achieve a lifelong dream.

When I was secured from Hellweek, that childlike ability to recognize my potential possibility was reignited in my soul. I knew that whatever I set my mind to was possible if I wholly committed myself to the task and accepted the fact that hard work is part of reaching any dream. I also realized that I was capable of so much more than I had ever imagined. My mind's inhibition was causing fear that overwhelmed my heart's desire. I made it through Hellweek because I anchored my heart to my mind.

Find your passion or dream and anchor it to your understanding of the incredible effort it is going to take to achieve *mission success*. This pure rational emotion will fuel your positive attitude like you have never felt before. This burning feeling will lift you out of the abyss of negativity you're drowning in and set you on a new course to achieving total mission success.

Step 2 - Start everyday Cold, Wet and Sandy

Wake up. Go straight outside. Turn on your hose. Douse yourself with freezing cold water. Lay down in a pit of beach sand or whatever you have outside. *Sugar Cookie* yourself from head to toe. Start your day. If you try this, AWESOME! If you don't, how will you ever know how it feels?

Cold, Wet and Sandy - *This is how students spend much of their time at BUDS. I once had a Wet and Sandy order given to me that lasted the whole week. This meant every time I reported into my Phase office to deliver the morning surf report I had to be soaking wet and covered in beach sand.*

Metaphorically speaking, what do I mean? Life is going to challenge you every day, especially if you want to make a real impact in the world. The problem with so many people is that when they face the slightest bit of discomfort it ignites a chain reaction that eventually leads to a small explosion of fear. This is why humans are so readily accepting of self-induced comfort zones.

In order to eradicate Comfort Zone Behavior you must get your physical, mental and spiritual self totally conditioned to function in any environment possible. This translates to being cold, wet and sandy. Why do you think SEALs are so successful? It's because we don't allow the normative concepts of rational fear or physical discomfort dictate whether we accomplish our mission or not. In fact, the more difficult the Op, or operation, is, the greater the feeling of excitement and accomplishment we feel throughout the mission.

How many times have you caught yourself getting bent out of shape when something goes wrong during your day? When your boss tacks on a little bit of extra work and you get pissed off because, in your mind, the work should have been delegated to the lazy knucklehead down the hall. Does this drive you nuts? What about when you get home at night and your pet has sprayed poo all over your room because you forgot to take him out that morning when you were running late for work? Felt like you're going to explode after this one, huh? How about something as small as someone getting your order wrong at a coffee shop? Does this turn your attitude into a giant mushroom cloud of negativity? Roger that!

Think about how you've been preconditioned to react the way you do in these annoying situations. From the time you were first able to put one and one together or tie your shoes, your training had started. Look back on your life and think about the repetitive negativity coming at you from all directions. It wasn't your greatest influences who taught you this behavior, it was the everyday people who played roles in your development. Your burnt out teachers. Your egomaniacal coaches. Your chemically depressed friends. Maybe even your uninspiring parents. These *lessons learned* shaped your conditioned emotional reactions or what world-renowned author and psychologist Dr. Daniel Goleman calls your Emotional Intelligence.

Check out www.danielgoleman.info for more info on Emotional Intelligence.

Lessons Learned – Critical life lessons you've learned from watching, living and feeling the impact of the world around you. These lessons learned can be positive and negative. It's your choice how they impact your life.

How you react to certain situations in life is entirely up to you. You need to train yourself how to feel and think in a way that is conducive to you achieving your dreams and forging your *Self-Confidence*. This all begins with ignoring your traditional comfort zones by embracing the feeling of being cold, wet and sandy. Once you've done this, begin a new and improved training regimen that involves having a positive attitude.

MISSION TIP:

Every time you say something negative drop down and do ten pushups or ten sit-ups. After a few days of doing this you will positively be forced to realize how negativity impacts your ability to communicate effectively.

Step 3 - Find A Swim Buddy

What is a *Swim Buddy* and why do you need one? A Swim Buddy is a person who you can absolutely count on to help maintain your positive attitude in the face of any adversity and someone who supports you on your commitment to living a *Team Life*. This is the human being who reaches out with a loyal hand and grabs hold of your battered soul and lifts it off the ground. A person who wipes the blood from your nose, shakes the dust of failure off your clothes and whispers in your ear to get back in the fight. A swim buddy will get *hammered* with you, laugh with you, cry with you and never turn his back on you.

Swim Buddy – A person that you can absolutely count on to help maintain your positive attitude in the face of any adversity and someone who supports you on your commitment to living a Team Life.

Get Hammered – Taking a physical or mental beating in relation to life's experiences.

There has never been a single person in history who achieved greatness alone. I challenge you to think of someone who has. We need others to reach our potential. That's right, these people in our lives play a massive role in our physical, mental and spiritual development. But you already know this. The real challenge is taking a minute to think about who in your life is making a difference by helping you become the person you want to be.

The key to finding a great Swim Buddy is being honest with yourself. What type of human being do you want in your life? What type of person do you need in your life? We've all heard the saying that *"you are who you hang out with."* Write down all of your friends that you believe have a positive impact on your life. Now write down all the friends who have a negative impact on your life. What does this list scream out to you? Are your current friends enhancing your life or bringing you down? Well are they?

	Positive		Negative
1.		1.	
2.		2.	
3.		3.	
4.		4.	
5.		5.	

In no way am I suggesting that your Swim Buddy must have the same objectives in his life as you do because that is very rare to find. Sure, having similar interests and hobbies is a plus, but by no means is it the critical requirement for the position. What I'm saying is that a Swim Buddy should be unselfishly fired up for you and want to be there for you during the successes and failures on your journey together. They should be in the trenches with you and not wishy-washy about facing the hard knocks of life. And the same is true for you. You should be totally committed to this pivotal living piece of lifesaving gear. In the Teams we say "take care of your gear and your gear will take care of you." Work as hard to build and nurture this relationship as you do in your effort to accomplish your dreams. Forge your positive attitude by constantly hammering away at life with your Swim Buddy. Easy day.

> **Easy Day** - Short for the SEAL motto - The only easy day was yesterday!

Step 4 - No Whining

Whining drives me nuts! It serves no positive function whatsoever in your ability to develop your *Self-Confidence*. I used to whine constantly when my *Self-Confidence* was suffering. Whining is a crack in your emotional armor. It allows negativity to fester like a wound and spread to other parts of your intestinal fortitude. It can infect your Swim Buddy, your *fire team*, and your *Team Life* platoon. And once the whining starts it spreads like the plague.

> **Whining** - The infectious negativity spewed out of someone's mouth when they have lost the intestinal fortitude to endure life's challenges.

How many times have you heard someone whining about the littlest things? "Why do we have to stay later? The other team hasn't done anything to help out the project." This type of commentary is like an insurgency against the potential success of you and your team. This presents a huge problem because of our cultural desire to jump on the bandwagon. Once a team member breaks down and lets out a whine, the potential for this grenade to be duplicated is

19

massive. It is the crack in the armor that other individuals are looking for to satiate their subconscious desires to submit to their own comfort zones. The next thing you have is momentary mutiny requiring a redirection of focus away from the task at hand toward dealing with the whining epidemic. I have seen this predictable behavior as an instructor countless times during training evolutions. When you start feeling tired or dejected in some way, your *Self-Confidence* will start to break down. Due to your preexisting comfort zones, in many situations you will allow this negativity to creep into your gut and eventually be forced to vomit searing hot negativity in the form of whining all over the place. And just like the real smell of vomit, once this proverbial stench hits the rest of the team, it initiates a chain reaction of blowing negativity chunks that inhibits the team's forward momentum. Nasty!

The truth about whining is that everybody does it. Even the most hardened troopers break down every once in a while and let out a whimper. The nice thing is that just like everything else in your life, it's easily preventable with proper training and disciplined dedication. Here's a list of a few physical and cognitive deterrents to this foul problem.

Physical:

1. As per the Mission Tip, every time you whine drop down and knock out 10 pushups or sit-ups. This positive, physical reinforcement will not only help get you into shape, but also link your negativity to a conscious open acknowledgment of your Comfort Zone Behavior.

2. Every time you catch yourself whining, add another five minutes to your daily exercise routine. Trust me, this will have a massive affect on your physical development. Eventually you will have accelerated so much in your workout capability that you will be ready for an ultra-evolution of your own.

Mental:

1. If you find yourself constantly bringing the team down with excessive whining, log all of this down on paper so you can cognitively understand the totality of this destructive behavior. Everywhere you go, carry a small Post-it notebook and pen. Each time you spew negativity in the form of a whine, mark it down on your Post-it. Keep a running tally of your negativity and at the end of your day count up all the times you broke down. After seeing the amount of destruction you are responsible for, I am sure your efforts toward developing your positive attitude will be reinforced.

2. Be sorry. If a whine slips out, don't be afraid to let your swim buddy or team know you're sorry. Apologize for your behavior and promise yourself it isn't going to happen again. Your internal cognitive effort will enhance your ability to accept this controllable lapse in focus and allow your Self-Confidence to remain intact. Remember, failure is a positive necessity in every aspect of our lives.

Be the cure for your team's whining epidemic. Confront this plague on all fronts. A healthy positive attitude is the best medicine for this disease. The faster you stop whining from taking over, the faster you'll feel better and the more self-confident you'll become.

Debrief

Having a positive attitude makes all the difference in forging your *Self-Confidence*. It is the initial spark that ignites that fire in your gut and enables your commitment towards fundamentally changing your human condition. You can be positive or negative. YOU CHOOSE how you're going to live your life. It is up to you how you're going to express yourself mentally, physically and spiritually. Nobody is forcing you to experience life in a negative way. If they are, shoot back with positive *effective fire*. Every day you wake up you should summon your intestinal fortitude the first time you look at yourself in the mirror. You don't have to open your laptop and download your attitude or even turn on the TV and have some news show personality blast you with a cup of sarcastic narcissism, starting your day with a negative mindset. Be self-confident and free to interact with your experiences in a positive stream of consciousness. Employ your new tactics. Anchor your heart to your mind and allow your heart's desire to manifest your cognitive dreams. Start everyday Cold, Wet and Sandy to erase your self-induced Comfort Zone Behavior. Find a Swim Buddy who supports you unconditionally and is there to pick you up when you fail and cheer you on when you succeed. Don't Whine and infect your team's ability to stay focused. You will immediately begin to feel a noticeable difference in your *Self-Confidence* and commitment towards living a *Team Life*. Easy Day.

MISSION 1: MENTAL TASKING

Instructions – Fill in the blanks below by providing honest and "Real World" answers. If you need more space, you can find something else to write on. Ready, Begin!

1. *Are you more often a negative or positive person and why?*

2. What childhood dreams have you accomplished in you life?

3. List the dreams you hope to accomplish in this lifetime.

4. What was the hardest physically and mentally challenging experience of your life?

5. How did you make it through this tough time and who helped you?

6. List your swim buddy or buddies and explain why they made the list.

7. Continue the list of negative "friends" you have and why they are in your life.

8. On average, how many times a day do you whine?

9. What are the top five things you typically whine about?

10. What is your plan to effectuate "Real World" change in your attitude?

Mission 2: PT and Live Healthy

Mission 2: PT and Live Healthy

Operational Objectives:

∞ *As you read this Mission don't get down on yourself for what you can't do, but instead get fired up about what you're gonna do!* ∞

Step 1 – Your Body is your Church

Step 2 – Booze and Drugs are Toxic

Step 3 – *PT* your Mind like your Body

Step 4 – Training Never Ends

Question – Are you happy with your body and mind?

∞ *This is a question you should ask yourself every day of your life. The two were designed to function together and not independently of one another.* ∞

PT Schedule:

5 minute stretch

25 – 8 Count Body Builders

50 – Stationary Lunges

50 – Air Squats

25 – Regular Pushups

25 – Extended Leg Crunches

25 – Regular Pushups

25 – Crunches

25 – Regular Pushups

25 – Crunches

25 – Regular Pushups

25 – 4 Count Flutter Kicks

25 – 8 Count Body Builders

It's time to *PT* (Physical Training)! Get your ass off the couch, exercise your body, and your brain will follow. You need to PT every day. Listen, I already know what you're thinking: "I am going to start tomorrow," or, "I really shouldn't over-exercise or I could permanently damage something." Well duh! Of course you should listen to your body's internal monitor, but don't allow what you think you're capable of doing inhibit your Real World physical potential. I am willing to bet that you could be doing a hell of lot more than what you're doing right now. When was the last time you worked out and felt like throwing up during or after you finished? If you can't remember, then something is WRONG! Pushing through the pain and fatigue is the greatest part of the entire process. Therein lies the true nature of discovering who you are, what you're made of and how much you can endure. These are the questions that you should be asking yourself when it comes to forging your *Self-Confidence*. Doing PT helps you to keep a permanent tab on this cognitive understanding and physical development.

You have to PT to be healthy. Your entire well-being is based on the combined health of your physical, mental and spiritual being. Your ability to endure life's challenges with *Self-Confidence* directly correlates with your health. The healthier you are, the better balance you have in life. The better balance you have, the greater likelihood you will achieve your dreams. There are countless studies that have proven your performance is linked to your cumulative health. Regardless of all the factual information, you know whether you're healthy or not. Nobody with any common sense needs some doctor or fitness coach telling them that they're out of shape. You are the definition of your own health.

Check out www.clinicaltrials.gov for interesting information on health.

Once again, as mentioned in Mission 1, *fear* is the leading cause of why humans don't aggressively pursue the development of their comprehensive health. So often people associate the achievement of physical, mental and spiritual strength with an unattainable timeline of hard work and pain. They lead with negative thoughts like, "This is going to hurt" or "This is going to take forever." These statements are just excuses. Excuses like these allow individuals to adhere to the complacency of their Comfort Zone Behaviors and submit to the fears of having to put forth an elevated effort. Excuses are devastating to your *Self-Confidence* and represent the habitual nature of your fears manifesting into reality.

Historical Debrief

In 1977, a quadriplegic young man with cerebral palsy asked his father to enter a 5 mile charity race to benefit a local Lacrosse player who had become paralyzed in an accident. An out of shape Dick Hoyt agreed to push his son Rick in a wheelchair for the entire distance. At the end of the race, Rick, using his face to communicate with a specially designed computer, gave his exhausted father the greatest gift of his life. He said, "Dad, when we were running it felt like I wasn't disabled anymore." Since that day the pair has participated in over 1000 races, including multiple marathons and 6 full Ironmans, as well as running and biking across America. The commitment these two men share for one another drives their internal desire past any possible fear of failure. The need to be healthy fuels their Self-Confidence to achieve total mission success, whatever the odds may be.

Check out www.teamhoyt.com

One of the most common *PT disorders* I see aside from simple excuses is the *Letterman Complex*. This is the person who psychologically attributes his or her current physical and mental fortitude to past accomplishments. Do you really think resting on the accomplishments of your past is going to keep your health at the level it needs to be? Especially as you begin to gain wisdom about the Real World, being the star player of your high school team doesn't mean squat 5, 10, or 15 years down the road. Sure, those successes play a role in who you've become, but it doesn't guarantee who you're going to be. It is critical to push past ancient history and embrace the challenge of being truly healthy now. GET OFF YOUR BUTT AND PT!

PT Disorder – *A psychological disorder that inhibits you from physically taking care of your body and living a healthy lifestyle.*

BUDS STORY:

Soft Sand Conditioning Runs were some of the hardest evolutions I experienced in BUDS. When I first arrived in Coronado I took one look at the beautiful, expansive beaches and smiled. I thought to myself, this is going to be a cakewalk. I was a former division one athlete and these beaches are huge (at low tide), what's the big deal? Right? Wrong, and halt!

∞ *Shaping your perspective to cover up reality is a sure way to fail. A great way to learn hard lessons fast, but no way to achieve your long-term goals.* ∞

My first conditioning run was a nightmare. It happened first thing in the morning at *O Dark 30* so I was already behind the power curve since I'm not a morning person. It was still dark and the mist off the Pacific Ocean was dampening our spirits as much as our clothes. We were all packed in formation like a bunch of sardines on the beach fidgeting with our canteens and *gig lines*, fearfully awaiting the instructors' arrival. We all tried to fathom the implications of our decision to volunteer and how we would fare during this

31

unavoidable *hammer session*, but couldn't have imagined what was ahead.

Hammer Session – A well thought out and planned beating designed to inflict just enough physical and/or mental pain to alter one's perception of their world around them.

As the instructors began filing in for the run I tried to guess who was going to deliver my voluntary pain for that evolution. I felt paralyzed as the fire in my gut cooled and turned to lead. Before I could mimic some of the other instructors' stretching routine, a tall slender gazelle-like man in a blue and gold UDT/ SEAL Instructor t-shirt shot past me in an angry blur. Within seconds I was sprinting down the beach through the soft sand, desperately trying to close the enormous gap that now existed in place of our formation. I was winded before I even realized what was going on. You could feel the panic spread throughout the class like a tidal wave.

Back and forth, up and over the 10 foot beach berms in front of SEAL Team 5 we went, trudging through the ankle to knee-deep crash of the shore line surf in front of NSW Group 1. Then, an all-out sprint to the rocks in front of the Hotel Del Coronado before this freak of nature showed any signs of slowing down. My heart and lungs were on fire. My thighs burned like nothing I had ever felt before in my life. No matter what I did, I felt like I couldn't gain any traction or pace on the madman leading this death sprint. As I gasped for air, all I could think about was this brutal "welcome" to BUDS.

Within the first ten minutes of running, the class was spread out across a mile of coastline. The collective unity of the class was destroyed as the weeding-out process began. Like blood in water, the massive group of students who didn't keep up with the front of the pack drew the instructors who were drawing the weak in for the kill. This defeated group was segregated into what is famously known as the *Goon Squad*. The Goon Squad was quickly ordered into the Surf Zone. The relief of the cold Pacific Ocean was short-lived as they were immediately forced into a make-shift formation and dropped down into pushup position. "Knock 'em OUT!" screamed the instructor as he led the self-inflicted torture. The pushups were quickly followed by an order to *Bear Crawl* back down to the surf zone. In an exhausted state, the Goon Squad followed the demands as best they could. "Flutter kicks, BEGIN," barked another instructor. By now many of the students couldn't perform a single pushup, much less the whole exercise. They had reached the absolute outer level of their comfort zones. When we thought it couldn't possibly get any worse, some of the truly ruthless instructors segregated a smaller Goon Squad to pummel them even harder. This was the hardest wake up call many of us had ever known.

Goon Squad – A group of students who can't physically or mentally meet the standards of a particular evolution. This group is then physically and mentally remediated during and after the evolution in order to motivate them never to end up in the Goon Squad again.

The top 5 percent of the class who had stayed within shouting distance circled together like a pack of Emperor

Penguins trying to protect themselves from an Antarctic storm. We kept our gasping heads down trying to ignore the hammer session going on no more than 50 meters away. I tried everything I could to slow my breathing and regain focus, but all I could hear was the constant psychological hammering coming from the medical support truck parked between the two groups. There was a running commentary being blasted over the intercom. It was a perverse diatribe directed towards the wilted mind of any student who listened. The instructor invected "Listen ladies, I am sure you never imagined that you were as worthless as you are right now. There is no shame in knowing that you aren't cut out to be a SEAL. Just get up, come over to the truck, ask to DOR and it's all over. You can go back to your pathetic lives. In fact I will help you find a new job in the Navy." Devastating.

BOOM! The gazelle was off again like a cannon. This Soft Sand Conditioning Run lasted for another 50 minutes until we had finally worked our way back to the PT platform in front of the BUDS beach gate. The Goon Squad was still in full swing when the lead instructor decided to combine the entire class in order to give everyone *full benefit*. We were collectively hammered to instill one of the greatest lessons learned in the Teams: *"You are only as fast as your slowest guy."*

Full Benefit *– The maximum amount of physical hammering an instructor staff can deliver before the net physical and psychological result ceases to be beneficial to the students.*

Over the course of the next 15 months I participated in many beach runs, never forgetting the impact of that first hammering. My final conditioning run of BUDS was a 14-mile formation run from Coronado to Imperial Beach and back. It was an amazing experience. We ran like *Frogmen*, wearing UDT Shorts and wet boots, singing the cadence of our past. "Up from a Sub, sixty feet below. Scuba to the surface and we're ready to go. Breast stroke, side stroke to the shore. We hit the beach and we're ready for war." We had all come to realize that the governance of *Self-Confidence* we yearned for resulted from a complete dedication to PT and a full commitment to living a *Team Life.*

∞ *You are going to take tons of beatings in your life, both physical and mental. The only way to endure and push past the constraint of your own comfort zones is to constantly test your physical, mental and spiritual strength.* ∞

Step 1 - Your Body is your Church

Your spiritual and mental strength is directly related to your physical ability. I don't care whether you're Christian, Jewish, Muslim or Hindu, we all bleed red. What matters in developing your *Self-Confidence* is whether or not you have a spiritual commitment to your physical being. Have you ever walked into a church and poured a whole can of Diet Coke into the wine cup? How about whipping out a cigarette and smoking a Camel Non-Filtered right in the middle of the sermon? Perhaps you were the one who stuffed your face with McDonald's every Sunday for a year during the service. This is insane behavior, isn't it? Then why do you treat your body any differently than you treat your faith? Everything you are is encapsulated in your body. Your body, your mind, the fire in your gut and your *Self-Confidence*.

You were given the most incredible gift known to human beings. YOURSELF! The nature of your intelligent design has kept humans on an upward spiral for millions of years. This was primarily due to the immensely difficult challenge of just staying alive. Now that we have dramatically altered this reality with Walmart Super Centers and McDonald's scattered around the world, we have generated a generational shift in life expectancy. Once the benchmark of survival was reached, the physical and mental fortitude of modern societies as a whole has taken a potentially lethal turn for the worse. The vast majority of the developed world has conveniently begun to ignore the simple truth behind our divine design.

Treat your body and mind with reverence and devotion. Put forth an effort to develop your faith. It's your faith that expresses your ability to effectuate change in the world around you. Your belief in yourself is driven by your physical, mental and spiritual strength. You need to exercise these strengths every day, otherwise they become atrophied. Forge this strength with exercise. Get outside and run along the beach during the sunrise.

Chase your best friend up the side of a mountain on your mountain bike. Swim across a lake that reflects the cobalt blue sky above. Allow this connection between you and the natural world to enhance your desire to PT. Fulfill the ancient prophecy linking your health to your quest for survival. It's time to build your church. Go PT.

∞ *Faith is a huge source of motivation for me. It fuels my fire knowing that there is something infinitely bigger than myself giving me the power I need to sharpen my body, mind and soul. Forge your faith in something.* ∞

Step 2 - Booze and Drugs are Toxic

I've never heard a success story involving someone who incorporates heavy drinking or drug use into his or her lifestyle. Sure, the mystique some people use is an illusion that this behavior is beneficial in some way, but in reality it's the eventual train wreck waiting to happen. We see it over and over again. Individuals thrust into the spotlight in some fashion eventually destroying their lives with horrific life choices. The pathetic thing is that this behavior is much more likely to exist in the "average Joe" than any public figure. Trust me. I know. I have come dangerously close to achieving the ultimate destruction of my life with the insanity of self-inflicted lies guiding my excessive indulgence.

There is nothing that destroys your *Self-Confidence*

more than the desire to incorporate booze or drug use in defining your character. I know what you're thinking: "Dude, why are you trying to rain on my parade? There isn't anything wrong with letting off some steam and partying a bit." You're right, there isn't anything wrong with a little partying. However, you know whether your lifestyle is healthy or not. When was the last time you blacked out and couldn't remember what you did the night before? When was the last time your intake effected any of your relationships in some way, shape or form? How about something as simple as your decisions to drink or take drugs always usurping your decisions to do something healthy? Be honest with yourself. Is your life guided by your desire to be intoxicated or by the emotional drive to make yourself a better human being? Well, what's the answer?

You have the choice. You determine what goes into your body. Dedicate yourself to putting the very best fuel into your engine. It pays huge dividends toward your ability to think clearly and perform physically. There is nothing wrong with a few spirits every now and then but make sure it never controls your cognitive or emotional decisions. Trust me, experiencing life with a sober mind is a million times more beneficial in your quest of forging your *Self-Confidence*. If you need proof, then try it. Replace the negative pattern of your toxic behavior with a positive commitment to living clean. You can do it. Just have faith that you have to do it. HOOYAH!

MISSION TIP:

Make a physical, mental and spiritual commitment to your PT. Set aside a time every day that is dedicated solely to your physical or psychological PT. I mean actually set a time like you set for eating. Create this constant in your life and watch your mission success happen instantaneously.

Step 3 - PT your Mind like your Body

DROP! Drop your brain down for pushups right now. How many did you do? Seriously, how much real cognitive PT do you conduct daily? When was the last time you learned something new that didn't apply to your job? You need to recognize that you don't know everything. In fact, what you think you do know has probably changed significantly since you last learned it. Life is changing so fast that it seems like an impossible task to keep up with everything. You're right. It is impossible to know everything, but that doesn't give you the excuse to abandon the need to better your mind with some intellectual PT.

Having a basic understanding of the world around you significantly enhances your *Self-Confidence*. Some of the greatest advice I ever received came from my father. When I was a young man he said to me, "David, the greatest way to travel through life is that of the Renaissance man." This has stuck with me since he said it 25 years ago. I've dedicated my life to becoming a cultured, well-traveled warrior who searches for answers in the beauty and pain of art, history, foreign affairs, adventure, music, religion, warfare, the physical and emotional forging process, teaching and love. This search has given me the power of knowing myself, becoming a *Warrior Poet* and living as a true human being.

Warrior Poet – A human being balanced by his or her reluctant willingness to fight for and defend the moral truth while sucking the marrow out of everything life has to offer.

What are some simple exercises for your brain? The easiest way I have found to PT your mind is to read. Activate your *neuromuscles* by sitting down away from all of the things in your life that will distract you. Turn off your laptop, lock your cell phone in a drawer and turn your TV off. Sit down in a comfortable chair and focus your mind on a story that will give you inspiration or knowledge. There are literally millions of books that can change your life. Who knows what story is going to inspire you to change your life forever?

Another amazing way to PT your mind is to create. It doesn't matter if you're creating a song on your ukulele or painting a picture of your favorite sunset like Bob Ross. Unlock your creative potential and explore what types of things make you feel good about yourself.

My wife creates something new in the kitchen almost every night. We are constantly exploring our taste buds with her phenomenal creations. She feels great when she discovers an awesome new blend of taste and textures. My young daughter exists in an almost perpetual state of learning and creativity. Her youthful innocence seems to be propelled by this incredible gift. And I am always working on some aspect of *Team Froglogic*. Whether I am editing a new motivational video or working on a new format for my instructional seminars, I am constantly using my creativity to express who I am and what I want.

The ability to create is a gift and should be exercised as much as your soul needs it. Remember how awesome it was as a kid when you could literally construct your own reality with a piece of paper or a set of wooden blocks? This is possible now if you let it happen. Express yourself and your dreams in order to create your future. My passion in life is fueled by the creative process and ignites my dream of touching millions of people to want to live with the same fire in their guts as I have. Use every creative tool you have to paint your masterpiece of your *Self-Confidence*. Create your life.

Check out www.bobross.com and learn how to paint.

Step 4 - Training Never Ends

Doing PT and living healthy is perpetual action that requires a lifetime of endurance and commitment. In the SEAL Teams we thrive on the never-ending quest of being the best possible warriors on the planet. Much like the Spartans of ancient Greece, we pride ourselves on a *Never Quit* mentality. This devotion to ourselves and to our teammates has created the Brotherhood that exemplifies the Warrior Poets of yesteryear.

Are you driven to be healthy or do you allow your self-induced comfort zones to warp your intestinal fortitude? If you answered yes, then, WHAT ARE YOU AFRAID OF? The pain? The suffering? The fatigue? The failure? All of these things are part of the forging process. Without experiencing each of these plus a slew of other physical, mental and spiritual defeats, you will never be able to understand what it truly takes to achieve a steadfast resolve. *Self-Confidence* is impossible without a healthy body and mind to support it. When you get beaten down by the hardships of life, it's the dense muscle tissue within your legs, arms, back and mind that are going to enable you to weather the storm. Trust me, your storms are coming. You can never totally escape the battering of the unknown, but with hard work and a never ending training regimen you will be prepared to clench your fist and scream at the top of your lungs: "Is that all you got?" once the lightening has gone. Training never ends. Period!

Debrief

PT and living healthy is the key to being able to endure life's challenges. Use your common sense as your conscience and be truthful to yourself about the status of you physical, mental and spiritual conditioning. Once you're able to admit your shortfalls, inspiration will quickly follow. Don't be afraid to initiate a regimen of healthy living because of the arduous amounts of PT awaiting you. Instead, welcome this forging process in good faith and commit to your revelation with religious fervor. Keep your spirit alive by rewarding yourself with controlled intake. Excessive booze and drugs will destroy your motivation and possibly your body if you allow yourself to compromise character with chaos. Don't forget that your brain needs just as much work as your biceps. Reinforce your effort with inspiration from others. Sit down and read a great book about another human being dedicated to effectuating Real World change. Create something new. Allow the child within to express a focused creativity and unlock you innovative spirit. And finally, this mentality can never end. Your effort should match the pace of your own heart. You can rest when you're dead. Never Quit!

MISSION 2: MENTAL AND PHYSICAL TASKING

Instructions - Fill in the blanks below by providing honest and "Real World" answers. If you need more space then go find something else to write on. Ready, Begin!

1. Are you happy with your body and mind?

2. What do you want to see in the mirror and feel in your heart?

3. How long did it take you to complete the PT listed above?

4. Do you have faith in your life?

5. Can you be faithful to yourself and live totally healthy for a month?

6. What are the top five harmful things you want to give up that are destroying your body?

7. How much booze do you drink a week?

8. When was the last time you took drugs and why?

9. When was the last time you lived totally clean and sober for a month?

10. Why do you use drugs or drink?

11. What was the last book you read?

12. What are the next 5 books you're going to read?

13. When was the last time you used your creativity to make yourself happy?

14. What is your training regimen for the next month, in detail?

Mission 3: Motivate Yourself & Others

Mission 3: Motivate Yourself & Others

Operational Objectives:

∞ *As you read this Mission allow yourself to get fired up. Stand up and let out a loud and thunderous HOOYAH if you want to.* ∞

Step 1 – Situation Dependent

Step 2 – It's Contagious

Step 3 – Be that Guy or Girl

Step 4 – False Motivation is Better than No Motivation

Question – What is driving you to succeed or fail?

∞ *Think about all the times you have done both and try to discover the answer that is always inside you.* ∞

PT Schedule:

5 minute Stretch

75 – Air Squats

25 – Stationary Lunges

50 – 4 Count Flutter Kicks

50 – Leg Levers

50 – Extended Leg Crunches

50 – Side Crunches

50 - Crunches

50 – 4 Count Flutter Kicks

25 – Regular Pushups

25 – Wide Grip Pushups

25 – Diamond Pushups

25 – Regular Pushups

10 – 8 Count Body Builders

I can see you right now, bombing down the highway in your beat-up, hand-me-down vehicle shouting Motley Crue lyrics: "Tonight, tonight, I'm on my waaaaay, just set me free, Home Sweet Hooome." It's amazing how some power ballad from your past can get you fired up and unlock the floodgates of emotional gunpowder. Maybe it's being out in the lineup and watching your swim buddy drop in on a huge 10-foot wave. Feeling that rush of physical and mental adrenaline pump through your veins is the greatest motivator in the world. Being able to ignite your neurological stimulus by conscious external stimulation that binds to your emotional drive is paramount in forging your *Self-Confidence*. Being fired up propels you to take hold of your life and lifts your *Self-Confidence* out of the ashes. When was the last time you felt that cognitive jet fuel emotionally inspire your actions?

Motivation is a fundamental component to developing your *Self-Confidence*. This is one of the greatest lessons I have learned. When I first became an instructor I realized that by first motivating my students, I was emotionally inspiring their cognitive commitment. Once motivated, they were willing to push themselves to achieve in any imaginable environment. This remarkable ability resonates into the phenomenal mission success the SEAL Teams have had over the past 70 years. For the past decade SEALs have been conducting covert operations in two of the harshest theaters Americans have ever fought in, Afghanistan and Iraq. *SOF* units have played significant roles in bringing democracy to these war-torn countries while staying motivated, deployment after deployment.

SOF - Special Operations Forces. This group is made up of incredibly self-confident, team orientated individuals who never give up and Never Quit! Units include the SEAL Team 6 (DEVGRU), 1st Special Forces Group Operational Detachment-Delta (DELTA Force), 160th Special Operations Aviation Regiment (Nightstalkers), 75th Ranger Regiment, The SEAL Teams (West Coast - 1,3,5,7, SDV1, East Coast - 2,4,8,10) Special Forces Groups - 3rd, 5th, 7th, 10th (Green Berets), Airforce Special Operations Command - 1st, 27th, 352rd, 353rd, 361st, 563rd, 720th, 724th Marine Corps Special Operations Command (MARSOC)

Historical Debrief

On December 25, 1776, George Washington lead a hungry and ill-equipped group of 2400 patriots on a secret mission that changed the course of the Revolutionary War. After suffering a great defeat and the loss of New York City, what was left of the Continental Army's morale was teetering on total destruction. Washington felt this sorrow among his troops and knew he needed to regain the momentum as enlistments expired and winter took its toll. He devised a daring plan to attack the Hessian garrison at Trenton, New Jersey. The Hessians were a group of brutal German mercenaries hired by the British. In order to gain the tactical advantage, Washington decided to cross the Delaware River in the middle of the night. The logistical challenges involved in successfully completing this move were historic. In the icy dead of night, with winds blowing freezing cold wind across the bows of their wooden craft, Washington's men, many of whom could not swim, executed their tasks with flawless devotion. The General was one of the first to cross the river, motivating his troops to embrace the running password of the operation: "Victory or Death." Washington and his men went on to defeat the Hessians at Trenton, and regained the motivation needed to carry them through the winter. His total *Self-Confidence* inspired his men to perform in the face of great adversity, thereby instilling the necessary motivation to achieve total mission success.

Check out www.mountvernon.org for more info on George Washington.

What motivates you? Is it a person, place, or piece of music? Perhaps it's a positive memory of you overcoming adversity in your life? Whatever it is, this is the critical spark that you need to light the fire in your gut. It is extremely difficult to go from 0 to 100 without any external influences. Try giving it a shot. Stand up right now, put this book down and go sprint around the block as fast as you can. GO!

That's what I thought, you're still sitting there contemplating the order because that's how you have been trained to respond in your life. First you make a choice and place yourself in a particular situation based on the requirements of your heart's desire or your motivation. Once you're in that situation, your traditional reaction to the external influences affecting your present experience are determined either by your Comfort Zone Behavior or your internal fears. So when forging your *Self-Confidence* it is imperative to learn how to push beyond your existing comfort zones to establish a whole new plateau of comfort. Additionally, you should embrace your fears by motivating yourself to translate your *flight* response into a *fight* response. Be ready to get knocked down, because the faster you motivate yourself to get up and get back in the fight of life, the stronger your *Self-Confidence* grows. HOOYAH!

Fight or Flight Response – a theory made popular by Walter B. Cannon, suggesting that all animals have a primal, sympathetic nervous response to external stimulus that enables them to fight or flee in an adverse situation.

BUDS STORY:

I met two of the greatest motivators I have ever known going through Boot Camp. John Zinn and Mr. B (still serving in the SEAL Teams) were 18 years old when we first met each other in June of 1995. In any other circle of society they would have still been considered kids. However, in our circle they were two of the most inspirational and hard charging human beings I had ever come across. They were fearlessly dedicated to their internal commitment of becoming Navy SEALs.

Not a day went by these two didn't talk about their desire to become Frogmen. Every chance we had we discussed our dream, constantly reinforcing our commitment. They had been driven towards this goal since they were kids. John had grown up in Southern California, swimming and working as a lifeguard on the beaches of Huntington Beach. Mr. B also spent a ton of time in the water swimming competitively since he was just a tadpole. Becoming SEALs was an absolute in their lives and it showed in their unwavering *Self-Confidence.*

After Boot Camp we spent several months at a major medical center on the East Coast waiting for our BUDS class to convene. During this time, John and Mr. B worked tirelessly at preparing themselves for the coming life-altering ultra-evolution called BUDS. Thankfully, they did everything they could to try to help me grow comfortable in the water. At that time I was a human barge in the pool. My fears were getting in the way of my ability to relax in the water. We practiced knot tying, drown proofing, underwater swims and logged thousands of laps in the pool. They were consummate team players and fed off each other's incredible motivation in order to help get me squared away.

When we finally reached BUDS there was a feeling of relief for all of us. It was time to put up or shut up. Unfortunately for me, after just a few weeks on the ground I suffered my first devastating injury. Due to the sheer amount and intensity of running, my ITBs (iliotibial band) in both knees were completely inflamed. I was unable to bend my legs without excruciating pain, much less run 6 miles a day to and from chow. I was medically rolled out of our class. This was a huge emotional setback to my *Self-Confidence*.

My personal motivation had suffered a major blow. It was horrible walking around on crutches while watching my buddies continue with training. John and Mr. B classed up and started 1st Phase with a comprehensive focus that was remarkable for two 18-year-old sailors. They charged every evolution like it was their last, providing endless motivation for each other and for their class. When most students struggled with the bare minimum, these two challenged each other to constantly better themselves. They weren't satisfied unless they had given it their all in every evolution.

My most significant memory of John and Mr. B occurred on the Wednesday night of their Hellweek. It was the dead of winter and this particular week was one of the nastiest in recent memory. Temperatures were consistently in the 40's and 50's with water temps in the low 60's and high 50's. The wind and rain on this particular night was unrelenting. Students often suggest that the BUDS Command Master Chief has a direct line to God. On this night it would seem that the call to hammer these boys had gone out.

It was the middle of the night when the class was herded past the barracks I was living in. The instructors decided to beat them just outside our windows. The sound of this beating was especially brutal. I decided to sneak a peek. I quickly found John and Mr. B among the group of exhausted recruits. There they were, backs straight in the pushup position yelling, "HOOYAH" at the tops of their lungs. They looked like they were having the time of their lives, living out their dreams in the worst possible conditions imaginable. They were totally stoked.

I was immediately inspired to let out a loud and thunderous, "HOOYAH" to their class, risking my own personal beating. Just as I expected, my two brothers echoed this call of respect with their own thunderous return. Their impenetrable spirit was exactly the motivation I needed to pull me out of my self-imposed funk and get back to achieving my own dream. The example set by John and Mr. B is precisely the type of motivation all SEALs use to accomplish mission success. Their internal *Self-Confidence* is directly correlated to their ability to succeed in living the *Team Life*.

∞ *True motivation comes from being in control of your life. The more control you have of your own choices the greater sense of accomplishment you will feel.* ∞

Step 1 - Situation Dependant

Every situation is different. Your life is a never-ending series of experiences involving different types of external stimuli that result in you acting and reacting according to the lessons you've learned in the past. Although no one experience is ever exactly the same, we do condition ourselves based on a variety of similar neurological and emotional responses that have proven effective in our lives. This internal catalog can be good or bad depending on how you have trained yourself to recall it. Often people recall Comfort Zone Behavior that generates the path of least resistance. Other times individuals are reactive based on fear. Those humans who have forged their *Self-Confidence* can typically rally an internal motivational spark that ignites their fire in the gut to overcome any positive or negative obstacle.

I am sure you have had some incredible experiences in your life, the kind where you called upon some type of motivational component to get fired up. In case you haven't, just remember back when you were a kid trying to go to sleep the night before Christmas or your birthday. That insatiable feeling of excitement that kept you up all night thinking about what presents you were getting in the morning was motivating.

The simple thought of being rewarded generates a physiological change in your neurological activity. In fact, all types of emotional cognitive input generate emotional cognitive output. These emotional responses typically effect your behavior, mood and temperament. Many leading psychologists and researchers agree on 8 basic emotions:

- Love
- Fear
- Enjoyment
- Sadness
- Anger
- Surprise
- Disgust
- Shame

Motivation can be applied in any situation in order to

enhance or combat whichever emotion is present. You need to generate a catalogue of different motivational tools for *Life's gear bag*. Whether it's a power ballad or an awesome memory of a great accomplishment, have something on standby to ignite your drive to succeed. After time you will be able to initiate your motivational mindset in any situation.

Life's Gear Bag – *The critical cognitive and emotional memories, thoughts, emotions and lessons learned that you keep stored in your mind. This gear is essential for completing all missions in your life. Take care of your gear and your gear will take care of you.*

Step 2 - It's Contagious

Just like a disease, motivation can be highly contagious, infecting people to react in such a dramatic way that their lives are changed forever. In fact, all types of behavior can be contagious. Think about all those people you know who need a huge dose of this behavioral treatment. Those eternally negative people who just can't find it within themselves to unleash the power of positive thinking and action. You can be the one who inspires another to alter their mindset and begin effecting change in the world.

Allow yourself to mimic the motivation you see. Don't sweat this. You have the ability to do this because it's a natural behavioral pattern within you. As infants we are initiated into this behavioral pattern as soon as we begin to gain some cognitive understanding of the environment around us. Just watch a toddler around other kids and his adults. Because humans are so predisposed for this, you shouldn't have a problem allowing yourself to be inspired and to mimic the people whom you believe have the most positive motivational focus.

The key to allowing yourself to be emotionally charged by someone else's influence is being resistant to your own internal comfort zones. Getting excited about something you typically fear and avoid isn't exactly normal behavior. Well, living your life in a dormant state of perpetual negativity isn't either. In order to forge your *Self-Confidence* you have to begin unlocking the emotional chains that typically restrain you from getting fired up about being alive. Identify the person who you believe has the natural gift of endless motivation and reach out to them. Become friends with him or her and see what makes them burn so bright. Try experiencing life as that particular person lives life. At first you might be a little uncomfortable, but suck it up, that's what this whole process is about. Changing your life patterns and retraining yourself to live with an unwavering motivated *Self-Confidence* is your challenge. HOOYAH!

Create a Playlist of five songs that ignite a different positive emotional response when you listen to each song. Always have that playlist available to combat negativity and ignite your motivational fire in the gut.

Step 3 - Be That Guy or Girl

We have all seen that guy or girl who comes out of the gates of life each and every day blasting off like a space ship. Bouncing off the walls, launching *verbal flash bangs* like, "DUDE, THAT IS AWESOME!" or "KILLER!" These are the people who live life every day like it's going to be their last. You need to be that guy or girl.

On the flip side of the coin, how many times have you heard someone witnessing this extremely motivated behavior say something like, "What an idiot!" Some negative turd passing judgment on another human being just trying to be positive is the most disgusting form of jealousy known to all humanity. It demonstrates the most vile characteristics of emotional insecurity. It is the form of fear that is the most detrimental for those trying to forge their *Self-Confidence*, because without a true sense of self many people will face this negative assault and regress back into their emotional foxholes. Remember, all behavior is contagious, especially fear. It takes thick skin and steely nerves to actually live life out loud.

When you first start trying this new style of living, practice it in small doses until you begin feeling your motivational strength harden. For instance, the next time you're among friends, make a suggestion to change the group's normative routine for the upcoming weekend. Plan an outdoor activity that pulls your friends outside of their comfort zones and forces them to experience the incredible physical, mental and spiritual impact of a natural environment. Lead them through this experience and don't allow any one negative comment to go unchallenged without a positive retort. You will begin to feel the power of effectuating Real World change in your friends and in turn will begin to feel your fears fade away and your motivational desire to be that guy or girl explode.

∞ *It's critical to remember that some people just won't change because you want them to. Don't waste too much of your precious time on those negative individuals or groups who just don't get it. There are 7 billion people in the world; find the human beings who do get it.* ∞

Step 4 - False Motivation is Better than No Motivation

Life is hard. I've been in thousands of situations where the *Suck Factor* is totally pegged. Those times where hope has faded and there is no end in sight. I am sure you have experienced these trying times as well. Maybe it was the last time you got in trouble with your boss and were on the chopping block. How about the last time one of your relationships was in the crapper because you both insisted on keeping score against one another? These nuclear times will test even the most hardened motivator. It's in these times when any type of motivation, including false motivation, is better than no motivation at all.

Suck Factor – A rating system for your physical, mental and spiritual status. For instance, when you have been getting hammered for 72 hours straight, the Suck Factor is high.

All it takes is one little comment, gesture, visual aid, memory or thought to turn the whole situation around. In my experience the greatest emotional penetrator is laughter. If you can crack a joke or tell a hilarious story right when the tension has reached its maximum level, more often than not, those involved will immediately respond to this levity with welcomed gratitude. Once you have altered the negativity of your emotional core with a conscious commitment to bringing a positive spin to your situation, then you have gained the upper hand on the gloom and doom of the situation.

Beneath every situation, regardless of its positive or negative nature, there is something you can learn from the experience. This process is simplified when you've been conditioned to embrace life's challenges by using an effective *PMA*, or Positive Mental Attitude. Staying motivated during bad times allows the memory receptors in your brain to generate neurological connectivity between positive emotional responses and the situation. Over time, you will be able to associate all situations with a motivational connectivity. So the next time you find yourself in a physical, mental or spiritual conundrum, shine some light on the situation with a little motivation, even if you don't really mean it at first. Easy Day.

Debrief

Motivating yourself and others is essential in forging your *Self-Confidence*. We are constantly facing the impact of a negative society thrusting its fear-based presence in our faces. You don't have to take it anymore. Every situation is different, so it's critical that you have plenty of motivational options to engage this enemy head-on. There are few of us who challenge these falsehoods every single day, so keep your head up and eyes open. Don't be afraid to ask for help and train yourself to mimic our behavior. Once you have practiced your new and improved highly motivated attitude, unleash it on the environment around you. Inspire your family and friends to throw off their chains of fear and live life every day like it's their last. And in the most challenging times, tap into your pre-conditioned response with a little laughter to get the ball rolling. Once you are eternally fired up, your *Self-Confidence* will bleed onto the people who mean the most to you. *OOUUTT!*

MISSION 3: MENTAL AND PHYSICAL TASKING

Instructions – Fill in the blanks below by providing honest and "Real World" answers. If you need more space write on something else. Ready, Begin!

1. *What drives you to succeed or fail?*

2. *List 5 of your greatest motivational failures.*

3. *List 5 of your greatest motivational successes.*

4. What situations do you perform best in?

5. What situations do you perform worst in?

6. Who are the most motivated people you know and why?

7. What is your plan for an exciting new weekend with your friends?

8. What was the last horrible situation you found yourself in?

9. How did you handle yourself?

10. How did you break away and what did you learn?

Mission 4: Earn Respect

Mission 4: Earn Respect

Operational Objectives:

∞ Self-respect and Self-Confidence are closely tied. It's mission essential that you recognize that earning the respect of others is also based on how you respect yourself. ∞

Step 1 - Don't Lie

Step 2 - Get Squared Away

Step 3 - Walk the Walk

Step 4 - Pays To Be a Winner

Question – Do you know your actions have consequences?

∞ I am sure you've heard about Newton's Third Law of Motion. With every action there is an equal or greater reaction. This applies to a lot more than just physics. Think about how your actions, words or thoughts play a in role in what happens in your life. ∞

PT Schedule:

5 minute Stretch

75 – Air Squats

25 – Stationary Lunges

50 – 4 Count Flutter Kicks

50 – Leg Levers

50 – Extended Leg Crunches

50 – Side Crunches

50 - Crunches

50 – 4 Count Flutter Kicks

25 – Regular Pushups

25 – Wide Grip Pushups

25 – Diamond Pushups

25 – Regular Pushups

10 – 8 Count Body Builders

As human beings, we are constantly searching for some form of acknowledgment regarding our actions. This response can be positive or negative depending upon how we insert ourselves into the world. It can be received in many different ways. We can feel it physically, mentally or spiritually. Perhaps the greatest way we feel this return of energy is in the form of *respect*.

Respect – *The positive emotional and cognitive recognition of yourself, another person or entity based on the specific or intended actions of those parties.*

Respect is one of the most sought out feelings any human being hopes to achieve in a lifetime. There are many different forms of respect when assimilating it to the cognitive desires of a person or persons. Historically, cultures around the globe have been governed by their ability to interact with one another. If respect is present, they have peace. If no respect is present, then they traditionally will war with one another. Present day societies are not much different than our ancestors. Enlightened cultures tend to define respect as a myriad of emotional patterns relative to one central core desire, the internal need to feel self-respect. Self-respect is based on the overt actions of others in response to your physical, mental and spiritual choices. However, there are still many warring cultures around the world that have chosen to adhere to their traditional philosophies and behavior. Respect is a common thread among all peoples.

How is this related to forging your *Self-Confidence?* From the time you are a toddler and begin to understand the basic rules that keep the natural order of human interaction in its fragile state, you are taught to believe that right and wrong is intimately tied to how people treat each other. You aren't supposed to punch another kid in the face because he has a popsicle and you want it. You shouldn't laugh at the kid who pees in his pants during recess. And you can't call someone a dirty name because she was laughing at you for being small for your age. I know these examples seem a little childish and simplistic to properly explain my concept. Here are some mature examples. You're out with friends at a bar and some jerk grabs your girlfriend's butt so you punch that person right in the face. How about passing quick judgment on a person with different skin color or cultural background as they pass you on the street? And let's not forget about the last relationship you had with someone and when it didn't work out, either you or your mismatch started spreading lies about the other. Isn't it funny just how similar adults are to kids? The point I am trying to make is that throughout life, emotional reactions, good or bad, are relative to how you internalize whether or not you feel like you are being respected or disrespected.

The greatest misconception spreading throughout much of the world right now is that respect is a given. Just because you walk upright and have opposable thumbs doesn't mean you automatically warrant the respect of others. Somehow over the last 50 years, several generations in many different cultures have been able to perpetuate the lie that everyone deserves respect simply because they exist. I agree that on some spiritual levels, all humans innately deserve a fair shot. However, the unfortunate truth about the Real World in terms of entitled respect is absolutely false. You have to earn the respect you desire.

Historical Debrief

On Thursday, November 19, 1863, a dedication took place on the hallowed battlefield of Gettysburg in Pennsylvania. President Abraham Lincoln delivered what many consider to be one of the greatest speeches in our nation's history. Interestingly, the President was not the keynote speaker on this somber day. It was Edward Everett, US Senator, Governor and Representative. Everett, who was considered one of the greatest orators of the day, spoke for two hours. Everett was followed by a sickly Lincoln whose speech captured the solemn magnitude of the battle and the War itself in a little over two minutes time.

"Four score and seven years ago our fathers brought forth on this continent a new nation, conceived in liberty, and dedicated to the proposition that all men are created equal. Now we are engaged in a great civil war, testing whether that nation, or any nation, so conceived and so dedicated, can long endure. We are met on a great battlefield of that war. We have come to dedicate a portion of that field, as a final resting place for those who here gave their lives that that nation might live. It is altogether fitting and proper that we should do this. But, in a larger sense, we cannot dedicate, we cannot consecrate, we cannot hallow this ground. The brave men, living and dead, who struggled here, have consecrated it, far above our poor power to add or detract. The world will little note, nor long remember what we say here, but it can never forget what they did here. It is for us the living, rather, to be dedicated here to the unfinished work which they who fought here have thus far so nobly advanced. It is rather for us to be here dedicated to the great task remaining before us—that from these honored dead we take increased devotion to that cause for which they gave the last full measure of devotion—that we here highly resolve that these dead shall not have died in vain—that this nation, under God, shall have a new birth of freedom—and that government of the people, *by the people, for the people, shall not perish from the earth."*

President Lincoln was able to command the respect of a Nation not because he spoke loudly or wielded his power with imposing dominance, but because of the words he chose to use and the empathetic manner in which he led the country. He realized early in his life that he was a servant for the greater good. In our nation's darkest hour, he made decisions based on the principles of humanity and not on the principles of power. History has chosen to remember Abraham Lincoln as one of America's greatest leaders not because of the battles he won, but instead for the human respect and dignity he fought for.

Check out www.alplm.org for more info on Abraham Lincoln.

Respect is earned. Your actions will ultimately warrant how you come to feel and understand the true nature of respect. The more you push yourself to walk the righteous path, the greater self-worth you discover. The greater the self-worth you weld to your actions, the more respect you will receive from the world around you. Once you realize that you have earned the respect of those around you, the stronger your *Self-Confidence* will be.

BUDS STORY:

My BUDS experience didn't exactly get off to an easy start. Within the first few weeks of my arrival I was facing my first medical roll due to inflamed ITB's in both legs. This meant I was unable to continue with my assigned class and was going to be rolled back to the next class. Thankfully, this option kept me in training and gave me two full months to recover. I saw a lot of great guys get medically dropped from training because their injuries were too severe to return without risking permanent damage and were too severe to medically justify keeping them in BUDS training.

After three weeks of rehab I was able to start training again. It felt great to get back to *PTRR* and with a class preparing to begin 1st Phase. I was so fired up to get things rolling. I made sure everyone around me knew how awesome and how lucky they were to be moving forward in BUDS. I was so motivated that I began doing additional conditioning after we were secured from training every day. There was no way I wasn't going to be prepared this time around. I usually ran an extra two to three miles in the soft sand each night. I figured this extra conditioning, combined with hard core Positive Mental Attitude, would forge an unbreakable spirit and body.

I remember the incredible feeling of starting day one of 1st Phase. I was finally getting an opportunity to realize my dream by knocking down the difficult days that lay ahead of me. It was an amazing feeling to be surrounded by men all crushing themselves to earn the respect of each other as well as the instructor staff. We were alive with the pain of dreams.

On Thursday night of that first week I went to bed feeling strong but ready for the break of the weekend. I had started to feel some pain in my feet just before hitting my rack but thought nothing of it other than just the standard daily pain of getting hammered in BUDS. When I awoke the pain had intensified significantly. I immediately began feeling fear well up inside me. I tried desperately to ignore the ache that was now in my legs as well. We mustered up as a class and prepared to run the mile to the *chow hall* located on the Naval Amphibious base across the street on the other side of the *Silver Stand.* As one of the road guards in class, I was responsible for making sure traffic stopped as our formation ran through intersections. This meant we had to sprint from one intersection to another, running *Indian Runs* the entire way to and from the chow hall. On this day, every step I ran felt like I had nails being driven into my lower legs. The pain was excruciating.

When we finally returned from chow I could barely walk. I had to do something I never wanted to do again in my life and request to go back to BUDS Medical to get my legs checked out. I knew this was my second time going to medical and most likely my last. Nobody ever gets double rolled for medical injuries. The instructor staff simply drops the student and moves on.

My request was granted and I left the class. I still had hope though. The DMO, or Dive Medical Officer at BUDS, needed to more definitively test to diagnose my injuries. I was sent across the street for x-rays. The walk across the street and the wait to be seen seemed like time was standing still and my future was hanging in the wind. I carried my x-rays back to BUDS medical in absolute disbelief that I was facing being dropped for something I worked so hard to prevent. I didn't understand why this was happening when I'd been so motivated and worked so hard to get back in training.

The results were conclusive. I had stress fractures in my tibias. The increased running had led to the breakdown of my bones through impact and overuse. The DMO recommended I be dropped from training and sent to the regular Navy Fleet. My dream was shattered again.

I was ordered to report to the Base Training Officer who would finalize my medical drop from training. I was consumed with an emptiness that felt like it would never be filled again. Before I reported to the BTO office, I returned to my gear cage to quickly polish my boots and tried to get my uniform squared away. I remember telling myself to hold my head high and act like a BUDS student should act. At that moment my military bearing was the only thing guiding my soul.

I knocked loudly and while standing at perfect attention I sang out, "Seaman Rutherford reporting as ordered, Sir!" The BTO said to come in. I removed my cover as I entered his office and marched to the center of the room. Standing as straight as possible with my chin tucked in and my chest out I tried desperately to give the appearance that I was not defeated and still had what it took to become a SEAL.

The BTO didn't say a word for what seemed like an eternity as he scanned my medical record. Finally, he looked up and with a smile on his face he asked a very simple question, "Rutherford, why do you keep breaking?" I was a bit taken aback by the jovial directness of his inquiry. I was expecting him to be angry or disgusted with my performance and for wasting his valuable time. I was wrong. With as much military bearing as I could muster, I asked permission to speak freely in order to explain my theory and hopefully get a chance to pitch my case for why they should keep me in training. He quickly snapped, "Rutherford, relax, stand at ease and tell me what's going on with you." I immediately complied with the order and launched into an explanation of utter confusion brought on by never having had a serious injury in 16 years of playing competitive sports. I quickly followed with the story about how I had conducted additional training on my own in order to prepare for this class. I pleaded my case and insisted that the injuries were a fluke and given one more chance, I wouldn't let him, the other instructors or myself down again. He paused for a moment as if I had touched a nerve within him. He ordered, "Stay here, I'll be right back," and then walked out of the office. Great, now I'm done for sure.

After about five minutes the BTO returned to his office. I came to attention ready to receive the news of my drop like a man. As he strode past me he insisted, "Rutherford, you have a BUDS angel looking out for you. I just talked to the PTRR Phase Officer and he thinks if you can stay healthy that you have the right attitude to make a decent SEAL someday. How much time do you need to heal? You can have a single or double roll. What's it gonna be?" I was in shock. I forced out a response and requested a double roll. I had just been given the chance of a lifetime because I had earned just enough respect from Warrant Officer Tom Rewierts to keep my dream alive. It was my *positive attitude* and the respect I showed my fellow students that made an impact on my instructors. If I hadn't honestly demonstrated these traits and earned that thin slice of respect, I wouldn't be writing this manual now.

∞ *Mr. Rewierts, I have not had the opportunity to say thank you for giving me the chance to realize my dream. Thank you sir.* ∞

Step 1 - Don't Lie

Lying is a guaranteed way to diminish the strength of your *Self-Confidence*, self-respect and ability to gain the respect of others. This concept seems like it should be pure common sense and everyone should be able to adhere to its simplicity. WRONG! Everyone lies.

The amazing thing about this truth is just how invested humans have become in the development of this particular skill set. People spend an incredible amount of time cultivating their abilities to lie to themselves and to others in order to make life easier. There are little white lies designed to ease the suffering of those you care about. Medium level lies intended to pump up your ego. And giant, cold hearted, Machiavellian lies designed to catapult you unfairly ahead of everyone else while satiating every possible negative desire you have along the way.

What I want you to do is to think about your life. How many times a day, on average, do you lie? I don't mean just the big lies but the little ones too. The lies that support your procrastination and unleash your excuses. When was the last time you kept track of your lying prowess? That's what I thought: you've never actually spent any real time quantifying your delinquency. I'm positive you've told a lie in some form within the last week. How about within the last 24 hours? Perhaps even in the last hour? Every time you tell a lie over the next seven days drop down and do ten pushups. Oh, you don't lie? DROP!

I'm not trying to suggest that you will never gain the respect you're looking for if you tell a lie now and again. What I am saying is that if lying becomes ingrained in your rhetoric, you won't be able to recognize the self-imposed disrespect directed toward you and your actions. Living a lie requires a perpetual negativity that blocks any possible development of your *Self-Confidence*. Does a self-confident, self-respecting person need to lie? Or are you lying because you aren't sure of yourself and you're afraid of what you don't understand? Remember, we aren't talking about some far out existential justification of your actions, we're talking about the simple truth behind your fear of not being respected. Your lies will never cover up the truth of fear; only your conscious desire to face your fears will result in the absolute realization of self-respect and respect that will inevitably be given to you.

∞ *A positive thing about utilizing physical discipline for actions is that you get fit correcting your negative behavior*

79

and you immediately feel better about yourself. ∞

Step 2 - Get Squared Away

Are you fired up to *Get Squared Away*? Awesome. That's what I hoped you would say. Let's take a minute to define just what getting *Squared Away* entails and how it affects your ability to forge your *Self-Confidence* and earn respect. Getting Squared Away requires a never-ending commitment towards doing the little things in your life that ultimately lead to emotional stability and cognitive focus. For example, take care of yourself physically by strictly adhering to a PT schedule that generates your physical fitness perseverance. Another example of getting Squared Away is making sure that you're challenging yourself mentally by exposing your mind to new and interesting topics. Finally, make sure your spiritual commitments play a major role in your life choices. These commitments, along with your comprehensive attention to the details, will ensure that your life is operating in a relatively positive manner. As a result, you will alleviate unnecessary fears that can interrupt the true perceptions of your surroundings. Projecting this sense of a Squared Away lifestyle correlates to how you will perceive others in their perception of you. Self-respect and the respect you receive from your family, swim buddies, teammates and friends is the result of working diligently on getting Squared Away every day.

Here are several Navy SEAL concepts and mottos to help you begin to Get Squared Away.

- Proper Preparation Prevents Piss Poor Performance.
- Attention to details.
- If you're not five minutes early you're late.
- KISS – Keep it simple stupid.
- Take care of your gear and your gear will take care of you.
- It pays to be a winner.
- The only easy day was yesterday.

These are some of the routine philosophies that the SEAL Teams live by. By adhering to these basic sets of guidelines, your actions will be representative of a human being that cares about himself and his teammates. You will find that the more you organize your life and reduce controllable uncertainties, your ability to present a Squared Away image is magnified significantly. This newfound preparedness will no doubt translate to you earning the respect of your teammates.

MISSION TIP:

If you aren't feeling the self-respect you want to have then do something for someone else. Reach out to someone in need and help him or her in some way. This selfless act will fill you with self-respect.

Step 3 - Boots on the Ground

There are a ton of phrases that have the same meaning as *Boots on the Ground*. *Actions speak louder than words*. *Walk the Walk*. And even *Lead from the front*. Each of these phrases, when used properly to describe an individual's effort, shows a strong sense of respect for that person. The inference is that well-respected people who embody this concept deserve credit because they don't talk a big game, they live one.

Boots on the Ground *- A term used to describe how a person's actions are directly representative of their statements.*

Life is filled with plenty of knuckleheads who spew out weightless commentary to enhance the perception of their own world. All too often we see politicians, entertainers, educators and our peers preaching to the masses about how awesome they are. How often do we witness those same individuals put their boots on the ground and truly effectuate change by doing the tough work required to make an impact?

It is true that words can inspire people to change. This is only possible, however, when the words spoken have been forged by true effort and relevant action. The inspiration we feel from hearing these words has a profound effect on our lives if we know it's true. Don't get me wrong, telling stories about the great accomplishments or hilarious antics of admired people is a great way to share emotional experiences. But when a person passes these exceptional exploits off as their own, it denigrates the impact of that action itself. It will also deter others from respecting that particular person and any future fable he spins. Be careful to lead with your actions and not with your words.

If you want to earn respect and feel a forged sense of self-respect, then put your boots on the ground. Get off your butt and take action. If you're not sure where to start, ask someone to help you get started. You can approach your church pastor, a non-profit organization, a charity, or even a local school and offer your services. Volunteering is a great first step in developing your self-respect and earning the respect of others. As you commit your time and effort for the benefit of the greater good, you will feel better physically, mentally and spiritually.

∞ *Remember, to earn true respect in your lifetime, your actions should somehow be directed at helping the greater good.* ∞

Step 4 - It Pays to be a Winner

I know, I know, you have immediately made the trivial jump to the movie Talladega Nights. The life motto that Will Farrell's character lives by, "If you're not first you're last." This is NOT what I mean when I say *it pays to be a winner*. Earning respect is a lifelong challenge and takes a tremendous amount of incredibly hard work. The more effort you make towards forging your self-respect, the greater probability you will receive the respect of others. When human beings push themselves beyond their personal expectations and begin to feel like they are winning at life, this emotional strength projects itself into their action or experience and ignites your teammate's willingness to project their respect for you.

Our society traditionally recognizes these accomplishments as great testaments to the human condition. We pay homage to those who totally commit their lives to accomplishing greatness. Olympic athletes, Nobel Prize winners, missionaries and charitable philanthropists all focus a major portion of their daily lives toward feeling that divine sense of winning. To win can be defined in many ways. I choose to define winning as a cognitive state of emotional elation governed by the ability to overcome adversity in any environment by pushing past any previously known Comfort Zone Behavior.

Competition is a powerful tool in our lives. It generates an internal desire to push one's self past a known point of internal comfort to a new emotional consciousness that enlightens our sense of self-worth and fuels our *Self-Confidence*. There's a small portion of our society who think that competition is bad. A handful of educators and psychologists believe that you are setting individuals up for long-term failure by accentuating the importance of winning. They say when a particular individual suffers loss repeatedly, it can lead to long-term emotional scarring. I say hogwash! Any action can lead to long-term emotional scaring if it isn't clearly defined and the intended lessons aren't tactically disseminated. It seems to me these teachers and shrinks should figure out a way to better prepare people for the competition of life and the healthy reality of failure instead of generating more excuses for humans to be okay with failure as a personal best.

Get out there and compete. Join a club of any kind where there are regular competitions and get your butt kicked. Failure is one of the healthiest forms of achieving success. In SEAL Training, students are constantly given serious doses of personal and team failure. This process is critical to developing a young frogman's self-respect and *Self-Confidence*. By getting back up after he's been knocked down it also helps him gain the respect of his teammates. This is how the Teams forge the bond of the Brotherhood.

Debrief

Earning respect takes years and years of hard work and patience. The process takes a lifetime of focused and sincere action. It is important to remember that you don't automatically deserve respect from your teammates, peers, employers, family and friends. Just because you have a pulse doesn't guarantee you a strong sense of self-respect. Every single day is an opportunity to prove your worth and value as a human being. Start earning the respect you're looking for by being truthful. Living a lie corrodes the strength of your resolve and weakens the power of your word. Get Squared Away! Organize your life and project a prepared and accountable lifestyle. This effort will increase the desire for others to want to work with you. The more you put your boots on the ground and let your actions speak for you, the more your teammates will trust your commitment to them and the mission at hand. Finally, push yourself to win! Allow the competition of life to fuel your dreams and watch your self-respect and the respect from others ignite your *Self-Confidence*.

MISSION 4: MENTAL AND PHYSICAL TASKING

Instructions - Fill in the blanks below by providing honest and "Real World" answers. If you need more space you can find something else to write on. Ready, Begin!

1. How can you tell if your actions have consequences?

2. Who do you respect most in your life and why?

3. How does this person live their life?

4. How many times a day do you lie?

5. How many pushup lies have you done today?

6. Who is the most squared away person you know?

7. Write down the upcoming week in a daily schedule.

9. When was the last time you volunteered your time and why did you do it?

10. List five possible charities or organizations you would like to help out.

11. Are you competitive and when was the last time you won something?

12. What does feeling like a winner mean to you?

Mission 5: Set Goals

Mission 5: Set Goals

Operational Objectives:

∞ Without goals, you lack a definitive direction to follow. Goals act as the GPS coordinates to achieving Self-Confidence in your life. ∞

Step 1 – Proper Mission Planning

Step 2 – One Step at a Time

Step 3 – Pay Attention to the Details

Step 4 – Debrief Everything

Question – Do you have a purpose in your life?

∞ Finding your purpose will enable you to lay out a set of goals to guide you on the right path of life. ∞

PT Schedule:

5 minute Stretch

75 – Air Squats

25 – Stationary Lunges

50 – 4 Count Flutter Kicks

50 – Leg Levers

50 – Extended Leg Crunches

50 – Side Crunches

50 - Crunches

50 – 4 Count Flutter Kicks

25 – Regular Pushups

25 – Wide Grip Pushups

25 – Diamond Pushups

25 – Regular Pushups

10 – 8 Count Body Builders

Setting goals in your life sets the framework for your physical, mental and spiritual dreams to come true. Without your own goals, you are allowing others to influence the direction you travel in life. This lack of control will act like a weight belt holding you down at the bottom of a pool. In order for you to be able to swim in the open oceans of life you need to have a plan to succeed and a direction to follow. These goals are critical to forging your *Self-Confidence*.

Historical Debrief

On April 28, 1980, a young man set off running from St. John's, Newfoundland. His goal was to run a marathon every day until he had run across Canada in order to raise money for cancer research. Terry Fox had been diagnosed with cancer which led to the amputation of his right leg. Due to the early discovery of his cancer, Terry was able to treat his disease and make what his doctor thought would be a rapid recovery. While going through his recovery process, he witnessed many other patients lose their fight with one of the world's most deadly diseases. This horrific reality and a competitive spirit inspired Terry to set a goal in his life to help the greater good by trying to raise awareness and increase funding for cancer research.

Terry's "Marathon of Hope" was little short of a miracle. In the beginning of his quest, Terry faced spectacular hurdles. He was met with foul weather and poor support, but ran through the problems and continued his quest with high spirits. He continued to gain traction with every aching mile. Soon people were turning out by the thousands to support this embattled journeyman, donating money and voicing their incredible inspiration. It wasn't long before Terry's story swept the nation.

By late summer he had captured the interest of thousands. When Terry Fox arrived in Toronto he was met by 10,000 supporters. Unfortunately, Terry's goal of reaching the Pacific would not be realized. Just outside of Thunder Bay, he was forced to stop because of serious heart pain. After being taken to the hospital he soon learned the disease had returned. Although his running days had ended, his quest continued. When Terry finally stopped running, he had raised $1.7 million dollars. But that wasn't the end of his giving. By April of the next year contributions had reached $23 million dollars, just three million short of his original goal of $26 million. His effort had inspired an entire country to make a difference.

Terry eventually succumbed to his disease and he passed away on June 19th, 1981. Terry is considered by many to be one of the greatest Canadians to ever live. In 1999, he was ranked Second Greatest Canadian of all time. His passion towards achieving his goals inspired so many through the simple act of running. There are no limits to what you can achieve as long as you have a goal and are willing to put the miles in to support that dream coming true.

Check out www.terryfox.org to get more info on Terry Fox's legacy.

Since childhood, you've been receiving guidance by those who want to help you succeed. One of the primary aspects of this effort has been getting you to understand the importance of setting goals, no matter how big or small. Remember those never ending reminders like, "Make sure to brush your teeth before bed" or "Get all your homework done before you go outside and play," that you were given as a child? These simple requests were the beginnings of your goal setting development. Nobody is going to ask a 5 year old for her 5-year plan. What parents, teachers and mentors are hoping to achieve by perpetually tasking their little operators is to generate an internal sense of cognitive commitment that results in repetitive success. The sooner you realize that the success of your life is highly dependent on the completion of hundreds of little *Life Ops*, the sooner you begin to feel the benefits from physical, mental and spiritual repetitiveness. Repetition is good. Repetition is good. Repetition is good.

Life Ops – *The endless little task or challenges in life that help you develop your ability to achieve mission success.*

As you've gotten older, your goal orientation has hopefully grown in scope and repetitiveness according to the types of dreams you have been aspiring to achieve. Or perhaps, like many other people in the world, you haven't really taken the time to set goals that represent the link between your heart and mind. Are you stuck in a lifeless job? Is your relationship floundering because you aren't inspiring your mate? When was the last time you got excited about executing your daily plan in order to succeed at something bigger than yourself? Without the perpetual regimen of goal setting in your life, the motivation to gain ground and make significant advancements in achieving your dreams is absent.

Life is tough enough without having a set of goals. Think about the times in your life when you were wandering aimlessly. When you lack the ability to meet the basic requirements of daily goal setting, you will meet trouble in many different areas. You will become an unorganized, slovenly procrastinator who always drags your teammates down. When was the last time you felt a real lack of drive or ambition? How did your laziness affect the people around you? Without goals in your life, there is no doubt in my military mind that you will not feel self-confident. In fact, down deep you will feel a sense of fear based on your inability to generate the physical, mental and spiritual momentum you need to move forward in your life. This is a strategic disaster in your Life Missions.

In the SEAL Teams, we are constantly generating new goals within our platoons and for ourselves. A day never goes by where there isn't some form of accomplishment happening. If an order is given and an individual isn't capable of handling the order, his entire platoon will contribute to that one man's success. The never-ending cycle of success fuels our forging process and solidifies our Team's *Self-Confidence*.

∞ *It is important to remember that it takes a real commitment to living a team orientated lifestyle to achieve the personal success you're looking for in life. Without living a hard core Team Life you will not achieve mission success. Period!* ∞

BUDS STORY:

Once I completed 1st Phase and Hellweek with Class 208 I felt like I was on a roll. I started 2nd Phase feeling invincible. My *Self-Confidence* was as hard as a rock. I managed my way through the first two weeks of *Dive Phase* unscathed by any testable evolutions. This portion of training consisted of much more academic work than we had gone through previously in 1st Phase. When we finally made it to *Pool Week,* some of my fears returned with a vengeance.

Pool Week in BUDS is considered to be the Hellweek of 2nd Phase. More students are performance dropped during this evolution than any other of Dive Phase. The week consisted of an escalating series of underwater evolutions all designed to test your comfort in the water. A SEAL's proficiency in the water is paramount, considering we are the premiere unit to conduct water operations around the world. Freaking out underneath an enemy ship or pier is not an option.

Monday morning was a shocker. You can imagine the nervousness pulsing through my body as our class was mustered on the cold deck of the *CTT* or Combat Training Tank. Once we received our Dive SUP checks, we waited nervously in formation. All 67 of us felt the gripping fear of not knowing what to expect once we entered the pool. The order was given to enter the CTT. As expected, after being in the pool for about twenty minutes, the underwater megaphone echoed in our brains and ordered us to the 3-foot section. We were instructed to sit down next to our dive buddies with our *Twin 80's* on our backs, backed up against the pool's edge. What followed next was pulverizing to my mental capacities, as I had just donned scuba tanks for the first time in my life. "Buddy breathing, begin!" It was horrible. Not only was I nervous as hell about using the old school twin hose regulators, but now I had to share my regulator with someone else. "Divers, start moving along the bottom of the pool towards the 15-foot section and be seated." Holy crap, I knew this was going to be a long week.

By Friday we had completed a series of testable evolutions that included Buddy Breathing, Ditch and Don, Night Ditch and Don, Buddy Ditch and Don, and finally Buddy Night Ditch and Don. Each of these evolutions is more challenging than the previous one. The skills required for completing these tests in the water further advance a student's ability to feel comfortable and learn how to count on their swim buddy in every aspect of a Combat Swimmer operation. I had a solid dive buddy, John, who always managed to motivate me right at the perfect time when I felt like I was going to drown. We ended up having a great week leading up to Friday's mega evolution, *Pool Comp.*

Pool Comp - A major testable evolution in 2nd Phase. This massive hurdle for students occurs at the end of Pool Week. This evolution tests a student's comfort level in the water under extreme stress. The instructors inflict four different types of problems within the students breathing loop, including the Wammy Knot.

Friday morning was the one of the greatest challenges I had ever faced. The night before I remember being inundated with overwhelming feelings about my future, my present and my past. The seeds of self-doubt were soiled into my emotional and cognitive psyche. No matter what I did I couldn't escape my mind and the negative wave of fear that swamped me. I had no concise plan of attack for going into Pool Comp.

At O dark thirty on Friday morning we had our Pool Comp brief. The evolution embodied every single aspect of mental and physical difficulty that BUDS had to offer. It was technically complicated, physically demanding, and required an absolute ironclad focus in order to complete the most grueling twenty minutes underwater we would face during this portion of training.

The run to the CTT was agonizing as I went over the Pool Comp procedures in my head, trying not to forget the proper order of the evolution and required action. Our class arrived at the pool and immediately disrobed and hit the *DECON Shower* for our traditional blast of cold water and mental reinforcement. We were ordered to begin preparation for the first set of divers to enter the pool. I wasn't in the first few groups to go so I sat impatiently as the worry slowly grew in my heart and mind. Finally, it was my turn to don my dive gear. After donning my equipment I moved to the waiting group of students mustered next to the pool edge. We were instructed to face the opposite direction, thereby making it impossible to gain any tactical advantage by seeing how the instructors were hammering the students beneath the surface. All I could think was, "Please don't let me get Chief Watkins, please don't let me get Chief Watkins." One of the instructors ordered me to turn and face the pool. The weight of my dive gear and anticipation of the evolution itself caused me to spin slowly. With my fins on I carefully moved to the edge of the pool and through the slight fog in my mask, I looked up and saw Chief Watkins eagerly waiting in front of me. He ordered, "Rutherford, enter the pool!"

It took 18 seconds after my first *Surf Hit* before I frantically signaled to Chief Watkins that I needed to surface. An instructor Surf Hit simulates what it might be like if a diver were caught in the surf zone getting slammed around the bottom of the ocean as giant surf washes over the *dive pair*. He started by aggressively ripping off my mask and fins and quickly followed by flipping me upside down and bouncing my face off of the pool bottom over and over again. It didn't take long for total panic to set in. All I could think about was getting to the surface and taking a breath of air. Chief was acutely aware of my frantic state and knew I was ready to surface. He forcefully pushed my face to the bottom of the pool as a reminder that I needed to begin my *free surface ascent* procedures so I wouldn't suffer an embolism as I rushed to the surface. He slowly guided me up, maintaining total control of my tanks as he assisted my exhalation by giving me a few pronounced gut shots to make sure I focused on not having an embolism because of my panic. As

I broke free from the depths of panic, I spit out my regulator and struggled to say the required statement, "I feel fine!" It was immediately followed up by Chief Watkins' response to my pathetic performance, "Rutherford, fail."

My poor performance continued for the rest of the day. I failed my second attempt with a slightly better effort than the first. The self-inflicted psychological trauma of my first try had taken its toll. I never recovered and was forced into a weekend of remediation training with the others in my class who had also failed. It was a long weekend. We repeated the correct procedures over and over again, simulating the exact events that had taken place on Friday. By Sunday afternoon I felt like I was ready to face the daunting task of going through Pool Comp again.

First thing Monday morning we were back at the CTT and again ready to face the impending hammer of Pool Comp. Today's evolution seemed to be moving at hyper speed because there were only a few of us getting retested. Before I knew it I was at the pool's edge, leaping into my own abyss of fear. Even though I had spent a ton of time over the weekend working on the exact procedures of the evolution, I spent almost no time setting a new set of emotional goals to help keep my fears in control. Almost immediately after entering the water I could feel my pulse quicken and my breathing accelerate. I managed to keep it together for three out of four of the simulated problems the instructor created for me. I ended up having to conduct a free surface ascent again during my exhalation problem. "Rutherford, fail."

It had come down to my final attempt. I remember telling myself to relax over and over again. I hoped this time all my fears would fade away and I would be able to focus on the task at hand. Unfortunately, like in life, it didn't happen the way I wanted it to. During my final problem called the *Whammy Knot*, I left the chest strap on my dive tanks twisted and signaled to my instructor I was done and ready to surface. When I breached the surface I sounded off, feeling pretty confident I had passed. The instructor was cool as he told me I had done everything correctly, except for the twisted strap. The emotional devastation was immediate. After exiting the pool, I sat cross-legged with my head down on the deck of the CTT with the seven other students who failed Pool Comp. A feeling of defeat swept across my horizon. I was positive that I was going to be dropped from training because of my failure to complete this major evolution. The fire in my gut had been extinguished by my own failures. I had lost focus on achieving my goals.

The following day the seven of us reported to the 2nd Phase office ready to receive our marching orders. Fortunately, because we all had exemplary records to date and because we all failed by missing only one procedure, the phase officer decided on extending our dream for just a bit longer. We were all rolled back to Class 209. HOOYAH!

During the two months the seven of us spent in PTRR waiting for Class 209 to reach Dive Phase, we redirected our focus on forging our *Self-Confidence* as it related to completing Pool Comp. We were given the opportunity to practice in the pool at the CTT every time our class went to swim. I learned to control my fear of diving and established a clear set of goals designed to help me complete Pool Comp. I was ready.

When Class 209 finally reached Pool Comp, I was more focused on achieving my dream than I had ever been in my life. I was one of the first students to enter the water. This time in I actually felt relaxed and excited about the impending Surf Hits. Fifteen minutes later I breached the surface and let out a loud and thunderous, "I feel fine!" I had completed every task with precision, displaying a focused comfort in the water indicative of a self-confident young Frogman. I had *planned my dive and dove my plan.* My strict adherence to achieving my established set of goals worked perfectly. "Rutherford, pass!"

∞ *Pool Comp proved to be the most difficult challenge I faced in BUDS besides Hellweek. I failed to go into the evolution with a comprehensive set of physical, mental and spiritual goals. As a result, it cost me two more months of getting hammered in BUDS. It was a lesson that still resonates loudly in my life today.* ∞

How do I set goals? Great question. It's easy. There are essentially two types of goals in your life, *Small Goals and Big Goals*. Small Goals consist of the Life Ops that help get you through your day and assist with the elemental breakdown of achieving your Big Goals. Big Goals are the *Life Missions* that guide your journey, giving a purpose to your path that enables you to feel a strong sense of personal fulfillment. Here is a *Froglogic Goal Setting Outline* to follow when establishing your new set of goals.

Froglogic Goal Setting Outline:

I. Life Ops: Daily and Weekly Small Goals

A. Timeline of daily/weekly goals.

Quantify the main types of small goals you need to achieve each day in order to feel successful. This should include the mundane aspects of your life that help you live a squared away lifestyle.

B. Break down achievement process in detail.

List the details of how you succeed in each Op or small goal. Be specific and include teammates that help you, time frames for each event and tools you might need to assist in completing your task efficiently.

C. Identify troubled areas.

What prevents you from achieving your goals? List the major problems or inhibiting factors that impede your success. For example, how much time you procrastinate or what types of things distract you. It could even be a recurring negative thought that always gets in your way.

D. Set new goals.

Once you've accomplished your goals be sure to immediately set new goals or similar goals to continue your momentum. Don't ever rest on the success of your last Op.

E. Try to perfect your process of achievement.

Don't repeat the same things that made you fail last time. The definition of high speed is doing the basics to perfection. Don't always feel like you have to reinvent the wheel, but make sure you realize that the wheel needs perpetual maintenance to keep on rollin'.

F. Debrief lessons learned.

Make sure you take the time to look at your progress and failures in a timely manner. Gaining immediate perspective will help you reduce the potential of another mistake and enhance your ability to achieve daily and weekly success.

II. Life Missions: Long term Big Goals

A. Timeline of existing and future goals.

Write down in detail your existing and future Life Missions. Explain why you have these goals in place and how they are going to help you achieve your dreams. Be as specific as possible and make sure you cover all aspects of your physical, mental and spiritual development.

B. Break down achievement process.

It is critical for you to break down in as much detail as possible how you're going to achieve your Big Goals. The more attention to detail you have the easier it will be to realize your dreams and forge your Self-Confidence. Remember to remain flexible because you will definitely need to revise your process again and again due to unforeseen positive and negative events that happen to you.

C. Identify troubled areas in your process and your behavior.

Don't ever try to ignore or deny problems that result from poor planning or a bad attitude. These things will simply compound over time and eventually derail your forward progress. Always be receptive to constructive criticism from your teammates. Be sure to take time for introspection and personal evaluation.

D. Set new goals or redefine the old ones.

If you get smacked in the face with a high dose of reality that leads to you failing at a Life Mission, well, guess what? Suck it up. It happens all the time. Life is tough. Murphy is going to rain on your parade every so often. The key is to reflect, reorganize and drive on. A significant portion of your life should be spent setting Life Missions and redefining old ones based on the never-ending experiences that shape who you are.

E. Try and perfect your process.

Life is constantly changing and so should you. There are a million ways to skin a cat but the challenge is figuring out what way is best for you. You are never going to come out of the gate with a perfect process in place. Constant adjustments here and there will enable you to reach your objective the best way possible.

F. Debrief lessons learned.

You need to realize that you're NOT going to accomplish your dream alone. Period! It is going to take a squared away team to help you get to where you want to go. Be sure to constantly get debriefs that should include constructive criticism and helpful advice. It is also very important to look inward at yourself and determine if you're achieving your dreams as a Warrior Poet would.

Step 1 – Proper Mission Planning

When was the last time you actually came up with a good plan? A hard core plan that changed your life? What made that plan so successful? Did you use a *phase line* approach or perhaps a *5 Paragraph Op Order*? If you can't remember or don't really have any recollection of such an event, then you need help. You need help generating a plan that is going to enhance the probability of achieving the physical, mental and spiritual success you desire. *Proper Mission Planning* will help you achieve your dreams.

---

5 Paragraph Op Order – A military planning strategy used primarily in small unit tactics. The 5 paragraph Op order breaks a mission down into 5 distinct stages of planning, ensuring units don't miss critical facets of any operation. Traditionally, they include the Situation, the Mission, the execution, Administration and Logistics and Control.

Proper Mission Planning requires you to have a guide or playbook to follow. If you don't have a guidebook then you need to find one immediately. The longer you *wing it* the greater probability you will fail at achieving your goals. Let me break down my system in order for you to see one way to knock it out.

Froglogic Mission Planning Outline:

I. Set a true Goal

    A. Something that you have spent a sufficient amount of time thinking about.

       Not some frivolous, spur of the moment idea or desire.

B. Commit to that Goal.

Make it the essence of your physical, mental and spiritual being.

II. Create a Timeline

A. This needs to be extremely detailed.

Breakdown as much as you can, to the hour if possible.

B. Set a *Drop Dead* date and time.

This forces you to complete it or reassess your efforts.
" I will be done on this date and time."

C. Make sure this timeline is a constant reminder for you.

So you don't let procrastination crush you.

III. Recruit your team.

A. Figure out who you need to help you achieve your goal.

These are specific people, not job titles.
Example - Joe Work is going to help me with PT every day.

B. Pick Teammates that have "Real World" experience where you need it.

Don't just pick a buddy because he makes you laugh and is a good mug.

C. Get Commitments from your Teammates.

These are hard core commitments that you can count on.

IV. Begin Training

A. You will need to train for this goal.

You don't know everything. Don't allow others to do the work you need to do for the Mission. Become an expert on your mission.

B. Don't cheat yourself on your training.

Train hard and train long. Don't ever say "I got it, I got it" and not know what you're doing.

C. Rehearsals, rehearsals, rehearsals.

Run through it over and over again. Play it out in your mind constantly.

V. Actions for obtaining your objective

A. Phase lines
   1. Beginning
   2. Middle
   3. Finish

B. Contingencies
   1. What ifs and Murphy's Law.

   Limit the amount of these so you don't go nuts.

   2. Prepare psychologically for them to happen. They will.

C. Reassess
   1. Plan Modification

   Find New Teammates and develop new training if you have to.

D. Objective Completed
   1. Drop Dead time reached.

   Don't allow yourself to keep pushing things to the right.

   2. Reassess

   In case of major catastrophes, create a new plan if needed.

E. Debrief
   1. Lessons learned

   Keeping a written record of your successes and failures is huge when it comes to setting new Life Missions.

   2. Thank You's

   Never forget to thank those who helped you reach your goals. It was and always will be a team effort. Live the Team Life!

   3. New Plan

   AWESOME! You made it! Pat yourself on the back and get ready to drive on. Create a new Big Goal and get busy livin'! OOUUTT

This Froglogic Mission Planning Outline should help you get started generating your Life Missions. The key to planning any great mission is to always remember to hold yourself accountable and remain flexible. The negative enemies in life will assault you with a constant barrage of fear tactics and demoralizing failures, driving you further away from your dreams. Stay true to hard dates and times and when something disrupts your plan, flow with it. Don't allow anger and frustration to deflect you from your plan. Roll with it, reassess and drive on.

Step 2 – One Step At A Time

Setting goals can be overwhelming in the beginning. It takes a ton of strength and focus not to get flustered with the gigantic ascension that lies in front of you. Take a deep breath and realize the process by which you are going to achieve your dream is what shapes you as a human being. The incredibly long hours you spend on reaching these goals are the best part of the effort. You will learn about your strengths and weaknesses. You will learn how to fail and what it takes to bounce back. You will learn about choosing the right teammates for living the *Team Life*. All these *lessons learned* are shaping and forging who you will become at the end of your journey. Take one step at a time and focus on the beauty of the moment.

Lessons Learned – These are the specific details that have the greatest impact on you from all the experiences you've had in your life. The joyful and painful memories that shape your perspective on life.

When I am facing the Über challenges of life I force myself to stop, reassess and embrace the right pace I need for the challenge. If I try to go too fast I cease to advance and start missing the lessons. If I go too slowly I just spin the wheels of complacency and never gain any ground. It is mission critical to break each portion of the operation down to its minutia. The pace of your effort is relative to the intensity of the job at hand. You should always feel a good deal of pressure, but not to the point where it cripples your spirit with fear or fatigue. During Hellweek I literally broke down every single order and tried my hardest to only think about what I was being asked to accomplish at that specific time and place. I didn't allow myself to think about the next evolution, or what was going to happen tomorrow, or even finishing the week and getting secured. When I did get weak, I was quickly reminded by my boat crew that everything is going to be okay and to just make it through that minute. And then the next. And then the next.

You always want to spend some time thinking about reaching your goal because it will fuel your will to endure whatever life has to offer. However, it can also break your will if you spend too much time thinking about your future success. If you combine the cognitive distance of reaching your goals with the physical and mental anguish associated with the fatigue, doubt and fear of achieving them, you're doomed. Be ready to initiate a *motivational trigger* that generates the mental explosion you need to disrupt negative thoughts and re-establish your direction. Achieving any goal is difficult without having these triggers in place. Make sure you have several motivational triggers to get you back on track.

Motivational Triggers - Anything that makes you feel awesome about where you are in life and grateful for just being alive.

Remember to embrace taking one step at a time. The physical, mental and spiritual strength you gain from this approach is certain to enhance your *Self-Confidence*. With each step, you gain small but significant victories. Even if you fail, that failure should resonate as a victory because you have just learned what not to do. Keep your momentum moving forward and allow patience to set your pace. This thought process is a proven way to assist in achieving your small and big goals.

MISSION TIP:

Whenever you feel like your life is out of control, STOP what you're doing, sit down and take some real time to rewrite your goals. The action itself forces you to focus your mind on something positive and gain some emotional and spiritual perspective on where you are in your life. The resulting plan will give you a new insertion point to begin operations again.

Step 3 – Pay Attention to the Details

How often do you have to have things repeated to you? How often do you get directions wrong or grow impatient when someone is desperately trying to explain something to you? How many times have you said, "I got it, I got it," and not really understood anything at all? There is nothing worse in this world than a person who doesn't pay attention and they think they know it all. Dealing with these obtuse, absent-minded people takes up way too much time. If the human race would spend five minutes more a day paying attention to the details, we wouldn't have half the problems we have in the world.

True knowledge is based around knowing the details. You've heard the saying, "knowledge is power." Working hard to gain a wide knowledge base has a tremendous effect on your feeling of self-worth. Your ability to contribute intellectually with sound, knowledgeable advice helps the team achieve its goals. If you don't know the details about something and still try to affect an outcome, you are most likely operating off of emotional intuition. In some cases this can be useful. In most, it creates confusion and problems. Spend time learning as much as you can about relative topics that will help you achieve your goals.

One of the main reasons why the SEAL Teams are so effective is because we pay an incredible amount of attention to the details. When people ask what makes the SEALs so *High Speed*, I always tell them that it has nothing to do with the cool equipment we use and everything to do with how we set our operational goals. We spend thousands of hours going over and over the little details that enable us to execute our missions with precision and flexibility. The definition of High Speed is performing the basics to perfection.

Stop for a moment and think about your dream. How much do you really know about all the steps it takes to achieve that dream? How many of those steps are a part of your plan of action? When you begin to really pay attention to the details, you will notice a massive change in your *Self-Confidence*. This happens because the unknown is erased from your thoughts, along with any type of fear that might hinder your forward progress. Paying attention to the details is absolutely essential to forging your *Self-Confidence* and achieving your goals.

Step 4 – Debrief Everything

When was the last time you screwed up really bad? I mean something that changed the course of your life. Maybe it was getting busted for being inebriated on the job. Maybe it was cheating on your significant other. What about getting arrested for breaking the law? Everyone has made mistakes in this life, some more than others. Unfortunately, it's the hard lessons that pack the most punch. The real question is, what did you do after that monumental error in judgment? Did you sit down and go over the experience again and again in your mind, following up with a written analogy of your mistakes? Did you reach out and have a teammate critique your blunder and give you advice on how to rectify your ridiculous behavior? Did you debrief your situation and tattoo the negativity of your behavior onto your soul as a reminder? Why not?

One of the greatest ways to relieve the pain of failure is to talk about the bombs that keep dropping on your knucklehead. This is another form of debriefing. Since childhood you have emotionally and cognitively searched for those loved ones who would welcome you with committed listening.

Hopefully your mom, brother or best friends would lift you off the emotional battlefield, patch your pride and refit your intestinal fortitude to get you back in the fight. When you've taken direct hits to your emotional armor, your perspective is often *fragged* with fear, anger, self-doubt and a slew of other inhibitors that shell shock your *Self-Confidence*. It's imperative to seek help. By not jettisoning this flak you simply move it to another cognitive bunker for storage. More often than not, this negativity will permeate to the surface and knock you off course from achieving your goals.

∞ *There is nothing wrong with getting professional psychological help if you can't find the answers with the help of your normal teammates. The most important thing is to get you back in the fight of Life, no matter what it takes. Never Quit! HOOYAH!!* ∞

In the Teams we minimize mistakes by maximizing our debriefing times. No person or Team is perfect. Period! Successful Teams simply reduce the possibility of failures better than the rest by setting clear goals. This is accomplished in part by taking the time to relay the lessons learned from an operation and disseminating the *Intel* properly. We also limit the finger pointing and embrace accountability, something that the rest of society is having trouble doing. *Passing the Monkey* is one of the greatest ways to enhance your Comfort Zone

Behavior and fracture your *Self-Confidence*. SEALs chalk failure or mistakes up to the realities of operating. We hold ourselves accountable by debriefing and then spend tons of time training to harden our fundamentals. Debrief everything.

Here is the minimum number of questions you should be asking yourself when you don't achieve your goals.

Froglogic Debrief Questions:

Positive

- *What made this mission so successful?*
- *When did I know we were going to succeed?*
- *Who were the major players in our success?*
- *What part of their effort was so critical?*
- *Why was I successful?*
- *Where do we go from here?*
- *How can we replicate our success?*

Negative

- *What really happened?*
- *When did it go bad?*
- *Who is responsible?*
- *Why did he or she behave like that?*
- *Where do we go from here?*
- *How do we get there?*

Debrief your day. Debrief your failures. Debrief your successes. Debrief your life. Your physical, mental and spiritual forging is dependent on momentum. Debriefing mitigates backward movement and facilitates the steadfast emotional and cognitive understanding required to gain that forward gain. It's the solid ground you need to march on. Allow those lessons learned to guide your goal setting decisions and achieve the dreams you desire. Mission success is dependent on the *Self-Confidence* you gain in order to soldier on.

Debrief

Setting goals needs to be a major part of your life. Your goals act as the rifling for your progress. It steadies your positive trajectory. Without goals, you won't be able to have an impact on the greater good which, in turn, negates the advancement of your *Self-Confidence*. Remember to delineate between the Small Goals of your daily Life Ops and the Big Goals that guide long-term Life Missions. Proper Mission Planning is essential. When you begin to lay out your plan of attack for achieving your goals, make sure you're using a method that works for you. Be consistent with your format and stick to the plan. Plan your dive and dive your plan. Always be aware that Mr. Murphy is looming and be flexible and ready to reassess your next move. The Froglogic Mission Planning Outline is a good place to start.

Once you initiate your plan, be patient and take it one step at a time. The process by which you achieve your goals is the learning part you need to forge your *Self-Confidence*. Constantly reassess your pace and make sure to feel just enough pressure to keep yourself on track. Pay close attention to the details of what you experience. It is the basics performed to perfection that make you most lethal at effectuating true change in yourself and your team. Take the extra time to learn as much as you need to become a measured player in the success of your team. Debrief everything, especially the catastrophic failures in your life. Don't stockpile unwanted fear that weakens the strength of your resolve. Mistakes are going to be made, but don't allow the same thing to happen twice. A massive part of your mission success revolves around the confidence you have in your understanding and ability to achieve your goals. Without goals you are wandering aimlessly, a ship without a rudder. Forge your *Self-Confidence* with clear goals and realize your dreams over and over again. *HOOYAH!*

MISSION 5: MENTAL AND PHYSICAL TASKING

Instructions - Fill in the blanks below by providing honest and "Real World" answers. If you need more space then find something else to write on. Ready, Begin!

1. What are your 5 most important daily or weekly Small Goals?

2. Where do you need the most work in your daily routine?

3. What are your 5 major long-term (3 to 5 yrs.) Big goals?

4. What type of Mission Planning system are you using?

5. If none, then apply your goals to the Froglogic Mission Planning Guide. Start your outline here.

6. Are you a patient person?

7. If yes, how can you apply that to achieving your goals? If no, why?

8. How do you typically learn things in the best manner for retention?

9. What are you best at? How did you get there?

10. What are the top 5 major screw-ups of your life?

11. Have you debriefed any of these in a comprehensive manner?

12. Who are your best debriefing teammates? Why?

Mission 6: Live with Integrity

Mission 6: Integrity

Operational Objectives:

∞ *This mission is one of the most important in your life. Living with integrity is essential to forging your Self-Confidence.* ∞

Step 1 – Right vs. Wrong

Step 2 – SA / Situational Awareness

Step 3 – Never Rest on the Success of your Last Mission

Step 4 – Never Quit

Question – Does Honor guide your behavior?

∞ *It is critical to first define what honor means to you. Then find some teammates or people who you perceive to have honor and try to replicate their behavior.* ∞

PT Schedule:

5 minute Stretch

30 – Regular Pushups

30 – Wide Grip Pushups

15 – Diamond Pushups

50 – Regular Pushups

25 – 8 Count Body Builders

100 – Air Squats

20 – Stationary Lunges

50 – 4 Count Flutter Kicks

50 – Leg Levers

50 – Extended Leg Crunches

50 – Side Crunches

50 – Crunches

50 – 4 Count Flutter Kicks

Mission 6 is one of the most important missions of all. Living with integrity provides you with a moral compass that keeps your declination on point and helps you stay on the right path in life. It governs your *Self-Confidence* and establishes a hardened set of rules to help you gracefully live the *Team Life*. There are tons of ways to define Integrity. In all the research I conducted I felt like Wikipedia defines this philosophical concept best.

" *Integrity is a concept of consistency of actions, values, methods, measures, principles, expectations and outcomes. In ethics, integrity is regarded as the honesty and truthfulness or accuracy of one's actions. Integrity can be regarded as the opposite of hypocrisy in that it regards internal consistency as a virtue, and suggests that parties holding apparently conflicting values should account for the discrepancy or alter their beliefs.* "

It is important to constantly define your concept of integrity. Without a personal definition, your *Self-Confidence* has nothing to adhere too. Think about how difficult it might have been writing the Declaration of Independence without the dream of freedom that inspired it. Integrity provides the human species with the repetitive consistency and accountability needed to ensure fair and equal outcomes amidst human interactions. If you don't act with integrity or if you have a substandard approach in your integrity, then your actions will inevitably cast rippled doubt and fear throughout your environment.

Historical Debrief:

John Adams was a man of integrity who had a profound influence on America and the way in which it was forged. His Puritan ancestors were some of the earliest settlers in the New World. They left England in a desperate attempt to find religious freedom in an unknown world. His father was a farmer and clergyman who instilled in his son the idea that integrity based on hard work and a moral interpretation of man's historical actions will give prudent guidance in any circumstance.

A young Adams diverted his father's hopes for a life of ministry and became a lawyer. He soon implanted himself firmly in the middle of Massachusetts's political issues of the day. His obsessive compulsion for acquiring the facts in as much detail as possible helped forge his reputation as a fair and adept counselor of the law. His rise as a public figure happened because of his notable resistance to the Stamp Act of 1765. In a series of anonymous opposition letters written to the Boston Gazette, Adams argued that the British Parliament was attempting to rule the American Colonies without the consent of its own legislature and far from any approval given by the people themselves. Adams maintained that the Stamp Act took away the two given rights of any Englishman: the right to be taxed only through consent of the people, and the right to a fair trial juried by one's peers. It was his dream of an integrity-based government that ignited the fire in his gut to be free.

Adams' acts of integrity are legendary along with his opinionated beliefs that sometimes got him in trouble with his contemporaries and fellow politicians. In fact, early in his career he defended British troops who were on trial for committing the Boston Massacre. His absolute belief in fair representation helped to get most of the troops acquitted and two of the shooters' charges reduced to manslaughter. For all of this he was paid the cost of a new pair of shoes.

As the relationship between the Colonies and the British deteriorated, Adams led the charge with his intellectual rebellion. Over and over again his carefully written words strengthened the resolve of colonial leaders. He was asked to represent Massachusetts at the first Continental Congress in 1774. Many historians believe Adams' sound judgment and spirited arguments for the succession from British rule was a catalyst for the rest of the Congress to agree on Independence during the summer of 1776.

The United States was born out of a cry for freedom and through the actions of brave, honorable men like John Adams, George Washington, Thomas Jefferson, Benjamin Franklin, Richard Henry Lee, Robert R. Livingston and Roger Sherman. Our founding fathers stood for something greater than themselves. They stood for governance of the people, by the people, for the people. In the opening two statements of the Declaration of Independence, co-authored by Adams, it states:

"When in the Course of human events, it becomes necessary for one people to dissolve the political bands which have

connected them with another, and to assume among the powers of the earth, the separate and equal station to which the Laws of Nature and of Nature's God entitle them, a decent respect to the opinions of mankind requires that they should declare the causes which impel them to the separation. We hold these truths to be self-evident, that all men are created equal, that they are endowed by their Creator with certain unalienable rights, that among these are Life, Liberty, and the pursuit of Happiness."

In these two verses the idea of American Democracy was born. Adams' integrity helped forge America's moral compass with his enlightened reasoning and insistence on fair representation. He served as George Washington's Vice President and eventually became the second President of the United States.

Although his political life was filled with controversy because of his opinionated resolve, his contribution and commitment to the United States is legendary. Late in life his integrity and insight can be seen in his correspondence with Thomas Jefferson, his long-time friend and political balance. The 158 letters give us insight into the brilliant moral minds of two of our country's greatest founders and leaders. John Adams will always be known for leading America to its freedom and helping to create its character by using his own integrity as his guide.

∞ You don't have to be a political revolutionary or democratic genius to have a massive impact in your world. Just be yourself and adhere to a moral compass that helps you live the right way and do the right things. Living *with integrity guarantees a strong Self-Confidence. ∞*

Think about your actions. Do you live your life honorably or do you justify your subjective honor by legitimizing the fact that the world is a jaded place? Having traveled the world, I've seen the very worst aspects of the human condition. Despotism, corruption and radicalism are just a few of the negative behavioral acts I've seen in my travels. Millions and millions of people worldwide are subjugated to the willful power of a few. The impact this has on humanity is so great that it has literally now begun to fracture our American ideals and principles. The *I Got Mine* attitude is being woven into our mindset at every level of our life. Once we get to college the insistence upon questioning authority has been taken to new extremes and allowed the sense of rampant narcissistic entitlement philosophy to corrupt our evolving cultural identity. The absolute cultural confrontation growing around the world is putting our integrity to the test. Is your behavior part of the problem or strong enough to effectuate a solution?

In the Teams, a major part of your reputation is built upon the perception of your integrity. This is especially true in BUDS, where your integrity is being watched with the precision of a laser range finder. Every single day your integrity is being forged and challenged. Whether it's related to a timed evolution or an ordered task, you and your teammates are expected to do the right thing. It is as simple as that. Lots of people make statements like, "If you ain't cheatin', you ain't tryin'." This is a ludicrous concept. There are way too many people who are cheating in every circumstance, hoping this will allow them to get by in the system. The only thing this does is fracture their integrity. Think about why we have rules or why standards exist. Think about all those who work hard to complete Life Missions using integrity and those who could care less about any moral code at all. This negative behavior makes it tough for the rest of us to walk the high ground. Once you subject your integrity to a lower standard and start acting like a knucklehead too, then you diminish your *Self-Confidence* as it relates to your ability to perform. Stay true to yourself and be self-confident to live life with integrity.

BUDS STORY:

One of the greatest beatings I ever received was because of my own lack of integrity. I'd recently been rolled out of 2nd Phase for failing Pool Comp. I was back in PTRR for the third time and not happy about this setback. My momentum had been halted by my own self-doubt and inability to set focused goals. Basically, the fear of Pool Comp got the better of me. As a result of failing I suffered a brief period of doubt that led to a momentary lack of integrity.

The day of my beating started out as ordinary as any other day in PTRR. We had a small group of *Brown Shirts*, those who had made it through Hellweek, and *White Shirts*, new recruits who hadn't even classed up yet. After returning from breakfast, we made our way out to the *O'Course*. As Brown Shirts, we ran the course first, demonstrating for the new guys the proper way to accomplish the obstacles. After running it twice we were allowed to leave the beach and return to *The Pit*. The Pit is a prep area that houses our outdoor lockers and affords recruits a place to congregate with a little reprieve from the instructors. This is an area for us to work on our gear, get our minds right, stretch or just mill about smartly. The Pit was our place to relax from the never-ending hammer of BUDS.

Once we were back at The Pit, I decided to take a little *combat nap* behind the lockers. The life vests used for Surf Passage were stowed and hung up to dry behind the gear cages. My plan was to camouflage myself with life vests as I slept, just in case any instructors came by to check on us. This seemed like a great plan for me to *get by* on the system. You see, it's absolutely forbidden to sleep during the training day. I figured we had nothing going on until lunch, why not get a little combat nap?

It wasn't long before a 2nd Phase instructor decided to drop by The Pit to check on the recruits. I was out cold and had no idea he was in the vicinity. It didn't take long before he spotted the toe of my boot sticking out from underneath the life vest. The next few minutes were a little blurry as he went *HIGH ORDER*. I remember struggling to keep my complete fear in check as he unloaded a fiery wrath on me.

You could literally feel the anger steaming off his breath as he yelled at me for being such a "Dirt bag!"

He decided I needed some extra attention for my blatant disregard of the rules. He ordered me to sprint down to the ocean, get wet and sandy, then bear crawl back to the pull-up bars on the beach. I have never run so fast in my life. As I reached the pull-up bars he ordered me to begin 8 Count Body Builders. As I attempted to complete each one with total precision he went into a fueled explanation of how my little combat nap represented a catastrophic failure of my integrity. After about twenty minutes of this he instructed me to begin pull-ups. Then Flutter Kicks. Back to 8 Count Body Builders. My hammer session lasted for an hour, as he instructed me on the finer points of Integrity.

When it was finally over I was mentally and physically exhausted. I felt totally defeated and knew I had let my team and myself down. As a Brown Shirt, I had a heightened responsibility to lead by example. My actions were directly responsible for lessoning the impact of training on all those around me. By breaking the rules, I was fracturing the strength of my *Self-Confidence* and was tearing down the commitment of my *Team Life*. This was one of the greatest lessons I learned in BUDS. Even the slightest pause in applying integrity to your daily life can have a massive impact on the success of your Life Missions. You are responsible for defining your integrity every day. When you start to disregard your accountability, you WILL get hammered. Trust me.

Step 1 – Right vs. Wrong

Do you know the difference between right and wrong? It's a simple question. Your answer has to be yes if you hope to forge your *Self-Confidence* with integrity. There is no excuse for not knowing the difference between right and wrong. You have been afforded plenty of opportunities to compile enough emotional and cognitive data relating to what our cultural belief systems define as right and wrong behavior. Our basic guidelines have mostly come from religious doctrine over the centuries. These Commandments are a great starting point to govern your decision process. Even with these, however, each day you're above dirt you should be physically, mentally and spiritually adding to these ideals. Your experiences help to cast your logical interpretation of living on the righteous path. You ability to adhere to these moral laws will enhance your *Team Life* and solidify your *Self-Confidence*.

Here is my interpretation of the Judeo - Christian Ten Commandments:

1. Believe in God

2. Don't believe in false gods.

3. Don't talk trash about God.

4. *Take at least one day a week to forge your faith. Give thanks every day.*

5. *Honor and respect your Mom and Dad.*

6. *Don't kill anybody, unless your way of life is under existential attack.*

7. *Don't cheat on or abuse your wife or significant other.*

8. *Don't steal.*

9. *Don't lie.*

10. *Don't feel the need to have other people's stuff. Earn your own.*

Real problems will occur in your life if you start to justify bad behavior by convincing yourself that it is O.K. to act like a knucklehead because everyone else is. This is the most common form of Comfort Zone Behavior that crushes your integrity. It's your responsibility to dial in your own moral compass. By allowing others to dictate your internal sense of retribution, you are passing the monkey. Of course it's easier to let the sometimes inadequate principles of people you perceive to be successful guide your behavior, because it essentially gives you the green light to follow their path. Anytime you absolve yourself of the consequences of your actions, you break down your *Self-Confidence*.

It is hard to walk the right path in life. I've struggled with it for many years. The truth is that if you take the easy way out, eventually you will have to face the music. The emotional devastation associated with the recognition of your immoral behavior and actions is so devastating, it could knock you so far off course that it takes years to get back on track. I am positive that you have strength to walk *The Jericho Mile.* You can face all adversity and adversaries that confront you with your physical, mental and spiritual faith as your shield. The greater your faith, the greater your *Self-Confidence* will be as you walk the mile, one step at a time.

Step 2 – SA Situational Awareness

You have probably heard the saying, "know your surroundings." Unfortunately, most people have little understanding of just how important this concept can be as it relates to the bedrock of your integrity and the development of your *Self-Confidence.* You are under assault every day from massive amounts of negativity. It is critical you understand how to recognize this insurgency. *SA,* or *Situational Awareness,* is the comprehensive ability to collect, assess, dismiss and act upon *real time* emotional and cognitive data resulting from the constantly changing external and internal environments that govern your physical, mental and spiritual experiences. Your SA is your understanding of the world around you.

Froglogic SA Color Coding: Based on Jeff Cooper's "Combat Mindset" coding system.

White – You are living with your head in the clouds. You truly believe that nothing is ever going to happen to you, or you just allow an oblivious attitude to dictate your Comfort Zone Behavior because you're afraid of acknowledging the truth about the Real World. You aren't seeing the potential dangers around you. You are living as an easy target, setting yourself up to become a victim of negativity.

Yellow – You are living with good SA and acknowledge that the world is a dangerous place no matter where you are. You are prepared to act in order to protect yourself. This includes being proactive in some type of training that diminishes your probability of becoming a victim of negativity. This easily attained SA is where you need to be on a regular basis.

Orange – Your Spidey senses are tingling and you perceive there is a threat of negativity in your vicinity. This heightened sense of awareness allows you to focus on the details that give you the advantage in case the situation gets worse. This attitude should not be maintained unless you have been highly trained to cognitively and emotionally handle the strain of this heightened SA. This means it is important to relieve this condition with assertive action and a positive attitude.

Red – You're going big! You have made the emotional

and cognitive decision to take offensive action to change your situation based on the real presence of danger. This is based on factual, negative environmental data focused in your direction. Your actions should be precise and explosive. Hesitation in this situation is not the deal! Once you are clear from immediate threats, don't downgrade your posture until you are completely out of harm's way.

Black – Some of us in the SOF community call this OBE: Overcome By Events. If you are incapacitated with this devastating inability to act, you will most likely be in the fetal position, sucking your thumb. This is where you DON'T want to be. It's up to you to never be in this position. You must take the appropriate measures and train yourself not to reach this paralyzed state. Life is scary and requires perpetual training to develop *Self-Confidence* in order to be prepared. Don't be a victim to a negative world.

∞ *Remember, developing your SA takes years and years of focused training and not lying to yourself about the true nature of the world around you.* ∞

How good is your SA? Do you walk around with your head in the clouds without a care in the world? This lackadaisical attitude is so pervasive in Western culture that it is no wonder we are facing such challenging times. When people stop caring about their actions and how it affects others, our society's future is destined for failure. I bet you can name at least three people off the top of your head who behave like this. We often mistake this for a lack of common sense or something as trivial as stupidity, when, in fact, what you are witnessing is one person's conscious disregard for the rest of us by ignoring his or her role in the interconnectivity of all life. The fact is that every action has consequence, no matter how big or small. Your actions reverberate throughout your world, forcing reaction among your teammates and enemies. How you choose to act is representative of your integrity. When you think before you act and proceed with the consideration of your teammates, then you are acting with integrity.

Froglogic SA Exercise:

Take two minutes to look around your room and remember as much detail about your surroundings as possible. Now get up and walk into another room. Grab a piece of paper and draw or list every detail about the room you were just in. Be as specific as possible. Describe or draw make, model, color, fabric design, height, shape, position, smell, age, history and emotional attachment of every item in the room. This exercise is designed to sharpen you situational awareness. Ready, begin!

Pay attention to your surroundings. Being obtuse is

no excuse for irresponsible behavior. Try to observe as much as possible. Watch how people are communicating with each other. Look for the subtle ways they interact because these signs are great ways to diagnose true intention. When you interact with someone, the tone of your voice, the words you choose and the emotional vibe you omit are all forms of communication. These expressions ignite other people's ability to gain SA of the situation. Sometimes you might need your swim buddy to give you a head's up when your SA isn't in focus and you're acting like a *knucklehead*. Remember, all things are connected through our actions. Another important part of having insightful SA is paying close attention to the material items that individuals collect, use and display. These things are an outward expression of what people think is important in their lives. What people wear, what they listen to, how they eat and where they live are just a few of the thousands of ways that help you gain SA on a teammate or adversary. The more details you can take on board as *actionable intelligence,* the greater amount of information you have to forge your personal sense of integrity. Once your *SA* is dialed in at a high level, you will feel a significant increase in your *Self-Confidence* because you are prepared to deal with any challenges you may face. Get your head out of the clouds and get your SA Squared Away.

MISSION TIP:

If you feel like your integrity is ever in question, be ready to ask yourself three questions: Did I act in an honorable way? Can I justify my actions and keep my integrity intact? Is it possible to fight for my honor without significantly degrading my integrity and the ability to achieve my dreams?

Step 3 – Never Rest on the Success of your Last Mission

Awesome! You just crushed your last mission and achieved a substantial goal in your life. Way to go, now get over it! How many times have you seen someone succeed and ride the wave of success as far as they can, making sure everyone knows they are in the position they're in because of a great accomplishment? This knucklehead lacks integrity. Listen, I'm not saying don't accept deserved recognition for hard work. What I am saying is that it shouldn't be the focus of your effort. A hard working person is a humble human being. A human being driven by the passion to excel and not by the desire to be acknowledged is quintessential for any life defined by integrity.

In May of 2011, SEAL Team 6 conducted the most successful raid in our unit's recent history. This incredible clandestine operation ended in the death of the world's greatest terrorist leader of our time,

Osama Bin Laden. This operation was a shining example of the incredible capabilities of SEAL Team 6 and our nation's intelligence organizations. Several days after the operation became public, I called a close friend of mine at Team 6 to congratulate him and the rest of the boys. At the end of our conversation, I asked him what the feeling around the command was like. He very eloquently stated that the guys were extremely annoyed because of the ridiculous amount of publicity being showered upon them. He continued by saying the only thing they really wanted was to get back to work and continue going after major threats to America. These are the statements and sentiments of men who live with integrity and are guided by the desire to help the greater good.

I am sure in the course of your life you have felt the allure of admiration or even desired a little fame. The emotional and cognitive influence of this condition is detrimental to the development of your *Self-Confidence*. The more pure and uninfluenced you are by the external materialistic perceptions of others, the greater your actions will be representative of the passionate commitment needed to succeed with humility. Once this is ingrained in your soul you will have no problems moving forward to the next great challenge and success of your self-confident life.

Step 4 – Never Quit

Never Quit. This is the greatest motto we have in the SEAL Teams. It is the DNA coding of our commitment to living the *Team Life*. Do you have this concept tattooed on your soul, or do you allow yourself to be easily deterred at the earliest sign of difficulty? Do you remember the first time you quit something? How did that feel? Do you regret your actions now? Quitting is the worst possible habit any human being can absorb into their defense mechanisms. It fortifies the most negative Comfort Zone Behavior there is and allows you to condone excuses in order to replace the effort of living with integrity.

There will be many times in your life when you feel like you're taking a perpetual beating, when everything you do seems like nothing is going your way and it seems like the easiest way to gain reprieve from getting hammered is to quit what you're doing. This is going to crush your *Self-Confidence* and pummel your integrity. Life is definitely hard, but this doesn't give you the excuse to give up. In fact, the beating you take is only making you stronger if you accept and embrace this reality. I spent 15 months in BUDS getting hammered week after week. For more than a year I was wet, cold and sandy. I can't even begin to tell you how many times I wanted to quit but I couldn't allow myself to give up. I just kept going back for more. Every pushup I did or mile I swam played a roll in getting me to where I am now, writing this field manual for you and trying to help you forge your *Self-Confidence* with the lessons I learned the hard way.

If you reach the end of a Life Mission without succeeding and you have tried everything, are you a quitter? No. The journey itself is the reward. Your life is going to be filled with a never-ending series of challenges that either strengthen your integrity or chisel it away. You will have experiences that don't play out like you hope they will. These positive failures are a part of your long-term development as a human being. It is critical to take these failures and apply them to your next mission. Achieving mission success is a relative concept. You might not become a Navy SEAL, but you will become a part of another unit that enables the Team to succeed. If you don't become CEO, then allow yourself to love being vice president. Maybe you don't become a professional football player, but instead you become a head football coach of a small college. It could be that you only make it half way up Mount Everest. As long as you give everything you have to the journey, you will eventually achieve something more significant than any title - your integrity. That is *Self-Confidence*.

Debrief

Integrity is an integral part of your life and acts as the moral compass for your actions. Living with consistency and a strict adherence to a core set of values will be challenging because all those who want the easy way out will be trying to influence your behavior with negativity. Make no mistake, if you choose to live a righteous life you will be assaulted by those who view you as a threat to their way of beating the system. It is critical to stay strong and focused on living a *Team Life*. Sometimes this task requires your effort to take a back seat to those who are the focus of the operation. Your time will come. Know the difference between right and wrong. How you treat others determines the power and strength of your integrity. It's the armor that protects your *Self-Confidence*. Keep a watchful eye on your surroundings. Don't let negativity penetrate your soul's perimeter. Pay close attention to those who love you. If you're acting like a fool, be available to hear this constructive criticism. There is no excuse for having poor SA. When you do succeed, be humble and appreciative of those who help you achieve mission success. Don't allow yourself to ride the wave of achievement too far. It's the journey that is your reward. If at first you don't succeed, then try again. Your integrity is tied to your ability to confront failure head on. When you get knocked on your butt you must not give up. Exhaust every possible option and learn from each mistake. There may come a time in your life when your dream is realized in a slightly different manner than you had originally imagined. Don't sweat the title. You have the strength to do anything you want. How you go about this journey is how you define your integrity. Never Quit.

MISSION 6: MENTAL AND PHYSICAL TASKING

Instructions — Fill in the blanks below by providing honest and "Real World" answers. If you need more space then find something else to write on. Ready, Begin!

1. *What is your definition of Integrity?*

2. *When was the last time your integrity was called into question?*

3. What were the last three honorable things you did for someone else?

4. How often do you allow your teammate's lack of integrity to go unchecked?

5. Where does your foundation of right vs. wrong come from?

6. What are your top ten rules that you try to live by?

7. How would you describe your situational awareness?

8. What type of training have you conducted to increase your SA?

9. When and what was your last great success?

10. How long from that success to the one before that?

11. How many times have you quit in your life?

12. What were the challenges that forced you to quit?

13 What can you do to stop yourself from quitting the next time?

Mission 7: Mentoring

Mission 7: Mentoring

Operational Objectives:

∞ *You will always need help forging your Self-Confidence. Because we don't know everything, we will always need mentors in our lives. For this reason it's critical to pass your wisdom on to those who need it too.* ∞

Step 1 – Nobody Does it Alone

Step 2 – If You Don't Know, Ask

Step 3 – We Never Stop Learning

Step 4 – Share Your Life

Question – When was the last time you asked for help?

∞ *I'm talking about serious help in your life. Not something trivial or simple, but asking for some hard-core life instruction.* ∞

PT Schedule:

5 minute Stretch

50 – 8 Count Body Builders

100 – Pushups

200 – Flutter Kicks

300 – Air Squats

"It takes a village to raise a child." You've heard this old African proverb a thousand times before, but have you ever stopped to think how many people have played a role in shaping who you are? Who are your mentors? Who are you mentoring? Have you ever thought about the responsibility you have in helping to mentor others around you? If it weren't for mentoring, there wouldn't be any dedicated *life instructors* or casual influences to show you the way. You wouldn't have someone to pass down critical information that ultimately shapes your *Self-Confidence* and teaches you how to live the *Team Life*.

Life Instructor - A moral, honest human being that tells you like it is based on their core desire to help you achieve your dreams. A friend and mentor that doesn't sugar coat life experience and holds you accountable for your actions.

A good mentor will have a tremendous impact on your life. This person will give you practical insight on emotional and cognitive perceptions based on his or her Real World experience. The challenge is finding a good mentor. The misconception is that there is a soothsaying wizard-like human being on every corner just waiting to help you on your journey. WRONG! It takes some real effort and focus to find a quality mentor. Be selective and understand that multiple mentors will enable you to get the most comprehensive life training possible. Here are seven qualities you should be looking for when selecting a mentor.

Froglogic Mentoring Criteria:

1. *Experience* – A mentor should have broad scope Real World experience. Having a firsthand understanding of the world gives a mentor a wide spectrum of experience to call upon. He or she should also have a positive specific understanding of the problems you need help with. Nothing beats gaining Intel from someone who knows the deal. Be leery of the know-it-all.

2. *Integrity* – Mentoring is a huge responsibility. It's critical that a mentor embrace this concept. Honesty is crucial when guiding another human being. Actions based on lies only lead to physical, mental and spiritual pain. A mentor should give sound advice based on how he or she acts in their daily life. When a mentor gives instructions that they don't live by, there is no truth behind their words and your bond. They should also be very up front when confronted with a problem that they have little or no experience in handling. Remember, nobody knows everything.

3. *Wisdom* – A mentor's ability to take Real World experience based on the totality of their environmental comprehension and translate that into sound guidance is the act of a wise human being. It's one thing to relate an emotional reaction to

a situation, but using wisdom requires a heightened understanding of life's complexity in its relation to long-term possibilities and outcomes. Wise mentors will give advice based on the long-term repercussions facing the mentee once the Intel is put into action.

4. *Resilience* – A mentor who has faced life's adversity and still maintains a Squared Away positive attitude is the type of person you want helping you. They should know what it feels like to fail over and over again but never quit on their dreams. They should know what it feels like to get knocked down, beat up and dragged along the highway of life. If you're getting advice to take the easy road then you're getting bogus Intel. People who lack a true understanding of suffering can't possibly identify with your struggles. Abraham Lincoln said it best, "Endeavor to persevere."

5. *Strength* - Physical, mental and spiritual strength are essential to instilling confidence in another human being. A mentor needs to exemplify these traits by instilling the necessity for the mentee to work hard on forging these aspects of their life. A weak body allows the fatigue imposed by stress and fear to break down the mind and spirit. A weak mind allows the influence of negativity to cause fear-based hesitation and procrastination to corrode one's dreams. A weak spirit allows the fear of the unknown to destroy your faithful commitment to your body and mind.

6. *Empathy* – Love is the greatest element of the human condition. Without it, your mentor will lack compassion and the ability to show restraint in times when it is necessary. Caring for the greater good should be the root of all action. As essential as this is, civilization has managed to break down this requirement at every possible level. A mentor should guide you after empathetic consideration has been made regarding the effect of your influential actions.

7. *Dedication* – Dedication to another person is most often seen among family, close friends and military units. Pick a mentor who has displayed the type of dedication in some other relationship besides the common ones. You want this person to be available and willing to help you even when you don't understand and resist their advice. Constructive criticism is imperative in the mentoring process. This isn't an excuse for you to act without integrity towards your mentor. Remember, this person is taking the time to help you achieve mission success in your life.

∞ *Everybody has different strengths in life. Find those who can help you with your biggest faults first and then move to improving your strengths.* ∞

These mentoring criteria are for you to follow as well. The greatest gift you can give someone is the truth as it relates to the testament of your trials and tribulations. Passing down lessons learned can have a profound impact on a human being who is in need of a mentor. Don't be afraid to embark on this journey. The reward you will receive is beyond description. When you are successful in helping someone navigate through turbulent waters, your *Self-Confidence* and commitment to living the *Team Life* reaches new levels of physical, mental and spiritual resolve. Try it today and help someone out.

Historical Debrief

In 1934, a young teacher decided to create his own definition of success based on his father's influence. His dad had preached to him three concepts to live by: never try being better than someone else, always learn from others, never cease trying to do your best. The young teacher defined success as a "peace of mind which is a direct result of self-satisfaction in knowing you made the effort to become the best of which you are capable." These lessons and definition were the foundation of John Wooden's coaching and mentoring philosophy.

John Wooden is considered by many to be the greatest basketball coach of all time and one of the greatest coaches in any sport. Wooden is most noted for his career coaching basketball at UCLA. He coached at the university from 1948 to 1975. In his final twelve years at the school, he won ten national championships, including seven in a row from '66 to '73. His lists of career accomplishments are astounding. He played at Purdue University where he won a national championship in 1932 and was named an All-American three years in a row. After a brief stint as a professional player, high school teacher and coach, he joined the Navy and served during WWII. After the war, he coached basketball, baseball and served as the Athletic Director at Indiana State University from '46 to '48. His continued success and notoriety blossomed and he was offered jobs at both UCLA and University of Minnesota. His tenure at UCLA is legendary. By the end of his career, he had been inducted into the Basketball Hall of Fame both as a player and coach.

Mr. Wooden was successful everywhere he taught and coached. His simple yet incredibly effective style of influencing the human beings around him to achieve their best was remarkable. His *Pyramid of Success* mapped a clear path for his students and players to follow. He devoted his life to helping others become well-rounded human beings. Think of the thousands of students he was able to inspire. In a 2001 *TED talk,* he gave examples of two players he felt had possibly reached their full potential while playing at UCLA. Wooden remembered both players were quite challenged as freshmen. By the time the two had reached their senior year, both starters were major contributors to the Bruins winning the National Championships. The young men, who many felt would never make the team, had a huge impact on their team and their coach. Wooden's players maximized their potential by embracing their mentor and committing the lessons learned to forging their *Self-Confidence* and living the *Team Life.*

Check out www.coachwooden.com for more info on John Wooden.

∞ Remember, discipline is a key to your success. If you fight this fact then you will be fighting your whole life. ∞

A good mentor will change your life. In the SEAL Teams, we are constantly evaluated by our chain of command. The constant ladder of evaluation exists so that every Frogman, from the time he enters BUDS to the time he retires, has members of his SEAL Team analyzing and guiding his performance. In BUDS this process is the most severe. During training a recruit's *Self-Confidence* is the most pliable. Without proper mentoring, students typically submit to the incredible pressure and challenges of life at BUDS. The initial forging process in your life will be difficult, too. You're embarking on a total change in physical, mental and spiritual thinking. Embrace your new life instructors full steam, and feel your *Self-Confidence* explode. HOOYAH!

BUDS STORY:

During my extended stay in BUDS I had the incredible opportunity of being exposed to a bunch of instructors who inspired me to push myself beyond my known physical, mental and spiritual capabilities. It was one of my swim buddies, however, who had the greatest impact on me.

When Hank checked in for class 208, I immediately knew we were going to get along. He was a little older and a hell of lot wiser when it came to understanding how the Navy worked. He was a Corpsman who had been a rescue swimmer in the fleet prior to coming to BUDS. Unfortunately, all of these attributes weren't good things in SEAL training. From the beginning the instructors *PINGED* on Hank for everything they could think of. Although he wasn't the most senior enlisted guy in our class, he was definitely the biggest lightning rod for the instructors.

What made Hank so inspiring was his unwavering *Self-Confidence* and his total commitment to his team. You see, Hank wasn't the shredded fitness nut you would imagine seeing in the Teams. At 5'8", he was shorter than most and his physical appearance was illusive. He didn't have six-pack abs and huge biceps. In fact, he looked like he was out of shape. Along with his appearance, his sharp wit and endless humor always seemed to draw the attention of the instructors. His appearance and attitude became the cannon fodder for our class, but he never broke down. He was one of the strongest performers in our class. He crushed ocean swims and destroyed soft sand beach runs. Pool evolutions like *Drown Proofing* and *Underwater Knot Tying* were just another day in the water for him. The only thing I ever saw Hank struggle with was an obstacle on the O' Course called the *Dirty Name*. His height made the leap from one log to the other extremely challenging. During one visit to the O' Course I saw him try ten times before he finally made it. Each time he flung himself at the beam, he slammed his ribs into the wood with reckless abandonment. Later we discovered he had impacted the wooden pole so hard he had cracked some ribs. He never complained and certainly Never Quit.

The combination of Hank's fearless, never say die attitude, and his endless sense of humor drove the instructors nuts. They singled him out for extra hammerings every chance they could. One of his duties as senior medic in the class was to report to the Phase office at the beginning and end of every training day to report which students were injured and which students had quit. The last thing any student ever wants to do is interact with the instructor staff more than absolutely necessary. He did it twice a day all week long and *paid the man* for it every visit. Every time he reported to the office he would be dropped down for a minimum of 20 pushups. Most times he ended up getting extra attention just for being Hank. Imagine doing an extra few hundred pushups, pull-ups or flutter kicks every day at BUDS. On more than one occasion he would return from his duties cold, wet and sandy as well. This never got him down. He always made light of the situation and used the beating as fuel to keep the fire in his gut burning bright.

Hank was unique in other ways too. He wasn't afraid to help a guy out emotionally. He was very insightful and would notice if one of his teammates was struggling with something. He had been around the block and knew what it was like to face real emotional adversity. His resolve and wisdom got me through plenty of times when I began to doubt myself. This isn't an easy thing to do in the SEAL community because you are constantly being judged by your ability to withstand the pressures of the job. Any crack in your armor might be considered weakness and potentially dangerous to the rest of the team. Hank was always there to help forge a swim buddy's *Self-Confidence*.

Hank and I went through some of the greatest challenges of our lives together. His focus and drive inspired me to be better every day. We lived together, we suffered together and we bled together. We shared the experience of being cold, wet and sandy together for 8 months. In that time Hank had such a profound impact that I still think about him often. His unbreakable spirit and impenetrable *Self-Confidence* were the influences I needed to make it through BUDS. Thanks brother.

∞ *Don't judge people for something as simple as their appearance or background. Give someone a chance to prove themselves before you decide that you have' em all figured out. You'll be surprised more than you think.* ∞

Step 1 – Nobody Does It Alone

I want you to name one person in history who's achieved greatness alone. You can't do it, because nobody has ever achieved total mission success without the help of a team. If you don't believe me then go Google it! The fact is we need Squared Away mentors to help us achieve our dreams. We need mentors to guide us, to teach us and give us *Self-Confidence* on the battlefield of life.

How many times throughout your life have you felt like you're all alone in the world when things just weren't going your way? I want you to think about the last time. I am willing to bet that you didn't seek out and find someone to give you an objective perspective on your situation. Too often we allow our pride or fears to get in the way of seeking help. You figure that after making it through a few hardships in your life, you've got a comprehensive understanding of how to handle things, right? The truth is, every situation is different and requires us to constantly ascertain new *Animaintel*, or soulful intelligence.

Animaintel – *The soulful intelligence one learns from others by allowing the intellectual breath of life to inflate one's soul with an infinite desire to physically, mentally and spiritually live a Team Life to its fullest.*

Mentors provide Animaintel. This vital philosophy helps you face your fears and find emotionally the driven, intellectual answers you need to achieve your dreams. The incredible teachers who inspire you to believe in your teammates are the greatest teachers of all. You are not alone in this life. Embrace the *Team Life* and experience the profound impact of how self-confident you become with this knowledge.

Step 2 – If You Don't Know, Ask

If you don't know something, then have the *Self-Confidence* to admit it. One of the worst sayings I've ever heard is, "Fake it until you make it." Do you really think this negative attitude is going to help you achieve the success you're looking for? Absolutely not. Eventually your teammates or enemies will find out that you have no idea what you're talking about. I am sure you've witnessed someone trying to pass bogus info in order make themselves look good. Do you remember what happened when the lie crumbled? Facing the music is part of life, but unnecessarily *bringing the hate* on top of your position because you were too afraid to ask for help is UNSAT!

∞ *Arrogance and ignorance are closely related. So are humility and honor. Which two do you want to have in your life?* ∞

If you're smart, you'll be asking for help for the rest of your life. There is nothing wrong with this fact of life. We live in the information age where answers to almost everything are literally a search engine away. Regurgitating facts straight off the Internet or out of a book can be useful and impressive, but it's not the same as asking for help from a real human being. That is why mentors play such an important role in your life. They can help you gain a personal insight into real world experience. A mentor can help you comprehend emotional and cognitive references and give them context. This is key when you're trying to develop your *Self-Confidence*.

From a very early stage in a young SEAL's career, he is taught the importance of asking for help. In BUDS, if a recruit tries to fake his way through an evolution there is a high potential for injury or death. The further along in training an operator gets, especially in a Platoon, the greater likelihood for getting himself, or worse, getting his swim buddy killed. It's the intensity and unforgiving nature of our job that forges this requirement. It also enhances our integrity. Having the guts to ask for help shows character and commitment to your team.

As an instructor, I always preach, "There is no such thing as a stupid question." I know you don't know everything and that's why I expect you to ask a ton of questions. And the same is true for your mentors. If they don't know the answer to one of your questions you should hear this statement immediately: "I don't know the answer to that, but if you give me some time I will find the answer and get right back to you" or "I haven't experienced that specifically but I have experienced something similar." It is important to remember that your mentors don't know everything. If you get bad *G2* from them, be objective. Your mentor has made mistakes in his life too. In fact, you might gain more perspective from his failures. By asking for help and paying attention to what you learn, you should feel a significant increase in your *Self-Confidence* when approaching the known.

∞ *There will be times when you realize the mentor you picked wasn't who you thought they were. Don't hammer yourself for making a bad choice because there is just as much to learn in our mistakes as our successes.* ∞

G2 - In the Army, an officer in charge of intelligence is considered the G-2 in the chain of command. This can also be used to describe any critical information that will help or impede your ability to achieve mission success.

MISSION TIP:

An easy way to identify a possible mentor is by making a simple list of the human beings you respect. Write down the top five people you feel meet the Froglogic Mentoring Criteria and play an active role in your life. Pick the top two and arrange a meeting with him or her. Be up front and ask if they will mentor you. Easy Day.

Step 3 – You Never Stop Learning

When was the last time you learned something new? Today? Yesterday? Maybe last week? Are you stagnant in your quest for knowledge? Do you average 5 or more hours of Xbox, Facebook, TV or smart phone usage a day? If so, you need help. Although helpful, the information you need to succeed doesn't lie in the virtual world, it exists in the Real World experiences that shape your *Self-Confidence* and understanding of what it means to truly live the *Team Life*. Our ability to navigate life successfully is dependent on the way we employ the knowledge we gain from living, not from the knowledge we download.

When you were young, hopefully a protective environment was made available to foster your ability to emotionally and cognitively ingest the fundamental knowledge provided from both academic and social instruction. If that wasn't the case for you, I'm sorry. However, even in the most terrible environments there are ways to learn.

There is a social order to our educational development in the Western world, and along with it, an expectation to apply your learned behavior in a manner that society deems appropriate. And once you've reached the culmination of your formal education, whatever level that may be, you are expected to enter society and sink or swim. This explosion of reality can cause a monumental shift in your ability to learn on your own. Without having someone to tell you what to learn and when to learn it, you might be intellectually stagnant. That is another reason having mentors is so critical to your success. These individuals help continue your education beyond sitting in a formal classroom.

Seek and you will find it. It is as simple as that. The answers you need in life are available if you choose to be patient and look for them. That's why mentors are awesome. Your mentor, if chosen correctly, will have some great insight on where you can begin to look for the answers you seek. In my life, my father has played a major role in helping to guide my journey. It's funny to think back when I was a young man and full of myself, I didn't realize the incredible wisdom he was bestowing on me. On my own, I suffered in many aspects of my life and career. I figured I could rest on my miniscule amount of life experiences to give me the right perspective on problem solving. Of course, my perspective was totally wrong and I paid the man for it. It took a long time and a lot of searching for me to wake up and see the answers that are right in front of me every day. Positive Mentors will never stop helping you to discover the answers you seek. To this day my mentors are still helping me learn new ways to improve myself and continue forging my *Self-Confidence*. Never stop learning.

Step 4 – Share Your Life

How detached have you become from the world around you? Do you spend more time reading emails or texting while you are in the middle of a conversation with someone? How often do you allow yourself to spend unrestrained time catching up with your family, friends or teammates? Time has become your personal insurgency, hasn't it? So many people allow the reality of lost time to impinge on their ability to spend quality time with the important teammates in their lives. Clock pressure has driven an emotional and cognitive barrier between the desire to share and the self-imposed need to answer the never-ending requests from the world around you. This narcissistic Comfort Zone Behavior is tearing us apart.

∞ *Time is a perception of your own doing. Don't miss the beauty of living life because you don't have time for it.* ∞

We are not supposed to live alone. You need to share your life. Our world is facing incredible challenges now because we have forgotten the importance of this human condition. Think about the incredible moments you've had in your life connecting to other human beings. Remember the physical, mental and spiritual strength you felt when you were there for your swim buddy or when they were there for you? The bond generated through sharing stories, eye contact, hugs and the ever so subtle nod of understanding is the warmth you feel in your gut. It is the fire that fuels your *Self-Confidence*. This is why we live - to share our lives with others.

Mentoring facilitates this critical aspect of human interaction. When you mentor someone and give them sound Animaintel that helps the person succeed, you feel stronger and more self-confident. When someone helps you succeed by sharing their lessons learned, your *Self-Confidence* breaks through all the pain of your own life because you know you're not alone. Throughout time humans have shared with each other. This is how we grow. This is how cultures forge themselves into societies and how civilizations endure. Control your time and share the *Team Life* with someone you love.

Debrief

Mentoring is essential in forging your *Self-Confidence* and commitment to living the *Team Life*. Our country and culture is built on helping each other succeed. A great mentor can effectuate Real World change in your life if you choose the right one. Stick to the Froglogic Mentor Criteria when searching for the person who can help you through the tough times in life. The same is true when you offer your insight to someone in need. Put away your fears and take a leap of faith when it comes to putting yourself out there. It's okay to need the help of your parents, coach, pastor, a family friend or even one of your peers. Nobody does it alone. You will always need someone to help you make sense of the world around you. Search for the right person who is able to share a legitimate philosophy or Animaintel. Don't let pride or fear inhibit you from asking for help. Have enough integrity to ask if you don't know something. Be willing to admit your limited knowledge and be accountable to find the best answer. For the rest of your life you have the opportunity to learn something new. Life has a funny way of changing course just when you think you have it all dialed in. Embrace this requirement and never stop seeking the truths about your environment. Once you've found these truths, SHARE THEM! This is not a me world, it's a we world. We succeed as human beings when we help the underdog, when the successful teach those willing to learn and when we all pitch in and work together in the face of adversity. Put away the stopwatch of life and pace yourself with the hourglass of connectivity. Positive Mentoring is the key to successful human interaction as it props up *Self-Confidence* and embodies the commitment to living a *Team Life*.

MISSION 7: MENTAL AND PHYSICAL TASKING

Instructions - Fill in the blanks below by providing honest and "Real World" answers. If you need more space go find something else to write on. Ready, Begin!

1. When was the last time you asked for help?

2. Who has had the greatest impact in your life and why?

3. Using the Froglogic Mentoring Criteria, briefly describe how each of the seven qualities applies to you.

4. How many people have you mentored in your life and what did you teach them?

5. What experiences in your life have given you the greatest Animaintel?

6. When was the last time you went at it alone and what was the end result?

7. Do you have trouble asking for help? Why?

8. Do you ever profess to know something you don't? Why do you do this?

9. What are you studying now and why?

10. What knowledge do you really want to gain and what is your plan to achieve it?

11. *Who is the smartest person you know and why?*

12. *Do you share your life with others? How?*

13. *Who is the next person you are going to mentor and why?*

Mission 8: Have Fun

Mission 8: Have Fun

Operational Objectives:

∞ *Being alive is a gift. Every day above dirt you should be living your life to its fullest and having fun while you're doing it.* ∞

Step 1 – Laugh it Off

Step 2 – Competition is Good

Step 3 – Take Risk

Step 4 – Love Yourself and What You Do

Question – When was the last time you had to pee your pants laughing?

∞ *Laughter is the fastest way to ease the pain of life and turn a negative situation into a positive one.* ∞

PT Schedule:

5 minute Stretch

50 – 8 Count Bodybuilders

25 – Regular Pushups

50 – Sit-ups

100 – Air Squats

25 – Regular Pushups

50 – Leg Levers

100 – Air Squats

25 – Regular Pushups

50 – 4 Count Flutter Kicks

100 – Air Squats

50 – 8 count Bodybuilders

Every day above dirt is a gift and an opportunity for you to have fun in your life. It's critical to forging your *Self-Confidence* that you understand the necessity of living your life filled with as much joy and happiness as possible. You've already discovered that life is hard as hell and it will constantly challenge your ability to endure failure and hardship. How you deal with these realities is entirely up to you. It's YOUR choice!

Take a minute and reflect on your life. Are you happy with who you are and what you do? Are you achieving your dreams? If you answered no to these questions, then I want you to ask yourself why? There is no good reason not to embrace life with passion and grace. I'm sure you've experienced pain, suffering, loss and fear in your life. It's impossible for these experiences not to take a toll on you at some point, but remember all these feelings are fleeting. The pain will end. The sooner you change your perspective and ignite your positive attitude, the sooner it gets better. The time you have in life is limited. Every minute you aren't having fun chasing your dreams is one minute you never get back. It's imperative that you understand this truth and complete this mission with passionate vigor; otherwise your *Self-Confidence* will get hammered. Your survival depends on it.

Historical Debrief

In September of 2006, a brilliant professor of computer science and human-computer interaction at Carnegie Mellon University in Pennsylvania was diagnosed with pancreatic cancer. Dr. Randy Pausch was given 3 to 6 months to live. Instead of retreating and accepting defeat from his disease, he did what he had done his entire life - he achieved another dream. Randy selflessly created a lecture entitled, "The Last Lecture: Really Achieving Your Childhood Dreams." On September 18, 2007, Randy gave his lecture at the University to hundreds of students, colleagues, family and friends. The talk was filmed and released on YouTube. The viral effect of this truly inspiring emotional and cognitive testament has been nothing less than miraculous. In The Last Lecture, he describes a list of childhood dreams that guided him through life, propelled his accomplishments, influenced others and effectuated Real World change for the greater good. Here is his list:

- Being in zero gravity
- Playing in the NFL
- Authoring an article in the World Book Encyclopedia
- Being Captain Kirk
- Winning stuffed animals
- Being a Disney Imagineer

In the Last Lecture, Dr. Pausch describes his journey of successes and failures as it relates to his evolution as a man and the eventual fulfillment of his dreams. He convinces us to believe that anything is possible through really hard work, working with great people and having fun. The truly amazing thing about his lecture is that a brilliant, personable, warm man on the brink of death is able to fuel our dreams through a very clear and intellectually lucid argument for having fun. Randy describes his Life Missions in terms of achieving dreams and having a very appropriate relationship, and vividly takes us along on his timeline. He maps out how his passionate effort and hard work taught him to become the man he was. In a masterful way he uncovers the eternal relationship between achieving your dreams and having fun while doing it. Randy's video and book have reached millions of people who needed to hear his message. I highly recommend both to you.

Check out www.thelastlecture.com for more info on Dr. Pausch.

∞ *There are millions of stories about great human beings overcoming adversity and living life to the fullest. Get off your butt and search for the ones that will inspire you to achieve your dreams.* ∞

Start living your life and have fun. Right now! Not tomorrow or next week, but today. Start making the physical, mental and spiritual changes necessary to truly live life as you should. First, get rid of all the negativity in your life. Write a list of all the negative things affecting you right now in your life. Now delete your negative attitude, friends, enemies, job and Comfort Zone Behavior by putting a black line through each one. If you have trouble identifying whether or not something is negative or not, use the *Froglogic Negativity Grid*.

The *FNG* is broken down like this. Identify something that you suspect is having a negative influence in your life. Using a one-week testing period with a 1 to 10 numerical rating system, plot how many times per week and at what level this negativity is affecting your life. If you are consistently ranking this person, work situation or Comfort Zone Behavior above 5, then you have an active negative threat in your life. If this negativity persists for more than a month then you have a downright negative insurgency waging war against you and your ability to have fun.

Froglogic Negativity Grid:

	M	T	W	T	F	S	S
10 SUCKS				X			
9	X				X		
8		X					
7							
6			X				
5						X	
4							
3							
2							
1 COOL							X

Negativity: Personal Fulfillment at my Job

Now that you have deleted some of the problems, it's time to move on. Let it go. If you can't let the negativity go, then I want you to ask yourself WHY? Is anything in your life really that *mission critical* to subject yourself to never ending negativity? The answer is no. Sure, I recognize that hard work and struggles are a part of succeeding, but not when it affects who you are physically, mentally and spiritually. If you're unhappy with what you're doing in life then it's time to change. Go find something in life that makes you feel great while you're getting hammered. HOOYAH!

BUDS STORY:

This BUDS story is about my entire experience. I was cold, wet and sandy for 15 months. I was in BUDS for twice the normal amount of time. Trust me, I wish I went straight through like a few of my best friends, but that wasn't in the cards for me. You see, I believe things happen in our lives for a reason. I believe I needed that amount of time to recalibrate my soul in a direction that would teach me how to use *Froglogic* every day of my life. I needed to forge my *Self-Confidence* and learn how to live the *Team Life*.

Right from the beginning the grueling physical and mental hammering seemed to get harder each evolution I did. The mental torture of not knowing what to expect out of training and myself was incredibly hard. Fortunately, life becomes fun when you and your swim buddies are cold, wet and sandy all day. The act itself is demoralizing but realizing there isn't anything you can do about it is enlightening and purifying at the same time. We were living our dreams. Even through all my injuries, a performance roll and all the stress of BUDS, I knew I couldn't quit. Something inside ordered me to keep going. It drove my legs forward, past the burn I felt during Soft Sand Conditioning Runs. It helped me ignore the horrific cramps in my feet during our Two-Mile Ocean Swims. It put a smile on my face while we were getting Surf Tortured in the ice cold waters of the Pacific. The painful reality of achieving my dreams was fun.

I was pursuing my dream that gave me purpose and no matter what was happening to me, I was having fun. I was having fun getting hammered by the instructors. I was having fun being scared to death while conducting night dives in Sand Diego Bay. I was having fun with the other men who were chasing their dreams, too. Our desire to forge our *Self-Confidence* and become part of one of the greatest teams on the planet was an incredible feeling. Every day we *knocked out* was awesome. Even though we faced constant failure, our bond grew stronger with each pushup, pull-up or flutter kick we did. We were having fun.

Frogmen have been subjecting themselves to this type of training, operating and elite lifestyle performance for over 70 years. Our lives are blessed with a mindset that doesn't allow us to do anything other than live life to the fullest. We succeed by using our *Self-Confidence* and commitment to living the *Team Life*. This confidence and commitment defines our ability to live a purposeful existence. BUDS was my indoctrination into this joyful mindset. I know it sounds crazy, but it's the truth. The hammer sessions and lessons learned have sharpened my ability to look at life as I should. Every day above dirt is a blessing. Every day you get closer to achieving your dream is a blessing. Every day you have fun is a blessing. Be blessed.

∞ You don't have to become a Navy SEAL to realize your dreams. You just have to be willing to get hammered and have fun while you define your purpose and chase your dreams. ∞

How are you going to make sure you have fun in your life? It's easy. The greatest thing about life is that you choose how you're going to live. You choose how you're going to approach your day. Are you going to be an emotional basket case and let every little thing get to you, or are you going to feel the beauty of the new morning sun as it hits your face? Let the sun fuel the fire in your gut. Wake up each day and take a breath of a positive life. Are you satisfied with how you're living right now? If not, then do something about it. Go climb a mountain. Write a poem. Throw a party for a friend. Have fun!

Step 1 – Laugh it Off

The easiest way to change a negative situation into a positive one is by laughing. Think back to the last time you were feeling like crap and one of your swim buddies cracked a joke or made a comment that made you laugh so hard you peed your pants. If you're laughing so hard you snort or get a stitch in your gut, life is good. Laughing is the greatest cure for being bummed out.

Laughing is one of the primary tactics in life for having fun. The more you apply this operational skill set, the better you'll feel. There are tons of hilarious things in life to laugh about, especially the behavior of our family, teammates and most often our enemies. Be careful not to corrupt this tactic by laughing at the expense of others too often. I've used the misfortune of others as an ignition point for my laughter thousands of times. It was mostly because I didn't feel good about myself. There's a problem with using the perceived failure of others as a relief to your own inadequacies. It's negative. The more you do it, the more you're infusing negativity into your life. If you want to laugh about something, laugh at yourself. Don't ever take yourself too seriously, that way you won't want to judge others to alleviate your own pain.

Surround yourself with laughter. How many times have you felt horrible and immediately pushed play on your playlist entitled "Sad songs to make me sadder" or "Hate music to enhance my anger?" Don't get me wrong, both types of music are good to listen too, but probably not when you're getting physically, mentally or spiritually hammered. The same is true for watching troubling movies or reading nasty things on the Internet. When you're beaten down, lift yourself up with laughter. Try and surround yourself with teammates who know how to get you emotionally Squared Away. Positive interaction between two human beings is the best way to get back on the right path of having fun. If nobody is available, then find something that will make you laugh. Putting a smile on your face with an uplifting song, movie or book is a sure way to turn things around in your life. Have fun, laugh and fill your soul with *Self-Confidence*.

∞ *Laughing is an important piece of gear for Life's Gear Bag, but it isn't the only tool you need. Acting like a clown all the time only makes you look scared. Sometimes life requires you to be serious. Have the Self-Confidence to know when it's that time.* ∞

Step 2 – Competition is Good

Competition is good and fun. When was the last time you raced your swim buddy down the street or joined thousands of people in a run for charity? How about the last time your team challenged another team at work to create a new idea or finish a project first? When was the last time you challenged yourself in anything? When you test yourself, you can begin to understand what your limitations are in life. When you know your shortfalls, it gives you a true understanding of what you need to work on. Without competition there is no way to know how you're doing. There is no benchmark to judge your success.

There are plenty of people who never compete or even want to. There are even people who believe that competition is bad for developing *Self-Confidence*. HOGWASH! When you compete, you fail. When you fail, you learn. When you learn how not to fail, you succeed. When you succeed and fail, your *Self-Confidence* grows stronger. Failure only becomes a problem when there is no learning attached to the failure. I have learned more in my life from failing than I ever have from succeeding. It was the times in my life when I allowed my failures to define me instead of inspiring me to try again that were not fun. My lack of *Self-Confidence* and fear of failure destroyed my ability to learn from my mistakes. Without the joy of competition in my life, I lost my ability to learn from my failures.

Get off your butt and register for a triathlon, golf tournament, writing contest or any competition that gets your blood pumping. It doesn't matter what it is, just find a competition and sign up today. Reverse the cycle of self-doubt and fear of failure in your life. Empower your *Self-Confidence* by testing your abilities against the world. You will never achieve your dreams without knowing what you're good at and what you need help with. That queasy feeling in your gut is good. It lets you know you're living life. Go put your uniform on, *kit up* and attack something with reckless abandonment. Feel the pure beauty of putting everything you have on the line against the masses. This is the fun of life. Life is a competition and the winner feels *Self-Confidence* because they tried.

> **Kit Up** - When SEALs or other SOF units get ready to conduct clandestine operations they put on their specific equipment needed to conduct the mission. They Kit Up.

MISSION TIP:

Find something that brings you joy every time you do it. Make sure you repeat this action at least once a day for the rest of your life.

Step 3 – Take Risks

As kids we took risks all the time. Sure, they weren't giant risks that had profound effects on our lives, but nonetheless, we still took tons of risks. Somewhere along the way, with each passing year you grew more and more cautious. The older you get, the more stunting your rationality becomes. Rational thinking is important, but very easily corrupted by the fear of failure and a negative attitude. I think the physical, mental and spiritual repercussions of failing trigger a carefulness that spawns the protective nature of your Comfort Zone Behavior. If you could only live with the excited curiosity of a child's mind! Guess what? You can. Taking risk in your life should be fun. Think of all the incredible experiences just waiting for you. Your ability to see new things, meet new people and feel great is entirely up to you. All you have to do is get excited and let yourself be free to try new things. Easy day.

When it comes to taking the big, gut-wrenching risks in your life, you're going to need some help. That's why you spend so much time recruiting a great team. Knowing you have an awesome team available to help you understand the comprehensive magnitude of the risk you want to take is huge in forging your *Self-Confidence*. Never be afraid to use your team as much as possible when deciding what to do next in your life. Your commitment to living the *Team Life* will pay off whenever you take a risk.

It is critical to understand that with every risk, there is a possibility of reward and failure. That's what makes life so interesting and fun. You never know how the world around you is going to react to your brave new attitude. Some days it's roses and other days it's the sewer. It is what it is. Taking risk lets you feel alive. It fuels the fire in your gut like a fresh wind to a fledgling campfire. The amazing thing about every risk you take in your life is that it brings you one step closer to realizing your dreams. If you don't ever take a risk, you'll never know what could have been. Trust me, have fun and take a risk.

∞ *There's a big difference between recklessness and risk. Don't sacrifice your Self-Confidence and commitment to living the Team Life because you want to be reckless.* ∞

Step 4 – Love Yourself, Love Your Team

Love is the most powerful physical, mental and spiritual force we know as human beings. Think about all the amazing and terrible things that we've accomplished in history because of Love. It has inspired artists throughout the ages to create beautiful works of art that fill us with hope and joy. Paintings, poems, books, buildings and songs have filled our lives with an endless source of fun. Think about the millions of charitable gestures made every single second around the world because of Love. The empathy we have caresses the sick, the poor and the needy with the touch of Love. Now look at the news and watch as people manipulate this miraculous energy to wage war against one another. During World War II, over 70 million people died because one man cajoled two nations into believing that killing was the loving duty of every man, woman and child. It has also hardened the resolve of countless last stands and given courage to honorable acts against oppression. Love is the foundation of every religion that has ever existed. It has given human beings a reason to live since the beginning. Love is the source of all your strength.

Love - An infinite source of power to forge your Self-Confidence. The positive power behind your commitment to living a Team Life. A gift from God.

Love yourself. Wake up every day and look in the mirror and feel Love. You are the source of your own success and loving yourself will enable you to achieve your dreams. PERIOD! You are worthy and capable of Love. Have faith in this truth. There is no doubt in my military mind that you will question this at some point in your life. I've questioned it many times. It's normal to question things in your life, but it isn't healthy to question whether you have Love in your life. It's all around you, you just have to open your heart to it. Once you feel love for yourself, then you can truly start loving others. Love your team. When you start to have fun with it, then it will start coming back to you like a perfect wave. Have you ever wondered why certain people feel love all the time? It's because they aren't afraid to put their Love out there. Don't try to contain this amazing energy that can change the world. Don't be embarrassed by showing your love for life and for your team. That's the craziest thing I have ever heard. Go ahead, stand up and shout at the top of your lungs, "I LOVE LIFE!" Let the greatest feeling and thought we have ever known take hold of your life and shape who you want to become and the dreams you want to achieve. *Self-Confidence* comes from Love. HOOYAH!

∞ *A dream originates from the love you feel for something bigger than yourself. Love will guide you there if you let it.* ∞

Debrief

Life is hard. It takes perpetual effort to keep your *Self-Confidence* strong. You're going to be cold, wet and sandy for the rest of your life, but that's okay. You now have *8 Life Missions* to help forge your Self-Confidence every day. A *Positive Attitude* will strengthen your ability to combat the perpetual onslaught of negativity brought on by the world around you. Doing *PT and living healthy* will give you the physical, mental and spiritual muscle to resist the fatigue of life. *Motivating yourself and others* will inspire you and your teammates to take on the world. *Earn the respect* you desire by acting like a true Warrior Poet. *Set goals* to guide your dreams and give your purpose direction. *Live with Integrity* and feel how honor can fuel the fire in your gut. *Mentoring* is how we learn the truth about what it takes to live a *Team Life. Have fun* and love the life you're living. Remember, all the *Self-Confidence* you want is already inside you. You just have to accept that it's your mission to face

your own fears. You've got your orders, now do it.
DO IT NOW! HOOYAH! OOOUUUTTT!

ENDEX - End of exercise. Mission Complete.

MISSION 8: MENTAL AND PHYSICAL TASKING

Instructions - Fill in the blanks below by providing honest and "Real World" answers. If you need more space go find something else to write on. Ready, Begin!

1. *What does fun mean to you?*

2. *What are 5 of the most fun times you've ever had in your life? Why?*

3. *Are you having fun in your life now? How?*

4. How many times a day do you laugh normally?

5. When was the last time you peed in your pants or had a side-splitting laugh? What was it about?

6. When was the last event in which you competed against other people? What was it?

7. Are you too competitive? Why is this bad?

8. What was the last big risk you took in your life? How did it work out? Why?

9. What are your biggest fears in life?

10. Do you have love in your life? What and who do you love?

11. What do you love most in life?

12. When was the last time love made you feel horrible? Why?

13. What do you love more than yourself?

Glossary

Froglogic (frog-lojik), n. 1. A way of thinking that perpetually activates an individual's desire to forge his or her own *Self-Confidence* in order to commit to living a team orientated lifestyle or *Team Life*. 2. A two-part motivational training program. Part 1 - Accepting 8 Life Missions into your lifestyle in order to forge your personal and professional Self-Confidence. Part 2 - Committing to 4 simple Missions that will ignite your understanding of what it means to live the Team Life. 3. A concept rooted in the proven experiences of over 65 years of UDT/SEAL "Real World" operations, training doctrine and elite lifestyle performance.

Navy SEAL – Sea, air and land commandos of the US Naval Special Warfare Command. Responsible for waging a non-stop campaign against all foreign threats to the United States and its allies by conducting clandestine operations around the world in every imaginable environment known to mankind.

1st Phase of BUDS – This phase is 2 months long and considered the *Hammer Phase* due to the intense focus on physical training and mental conditioning. The infamous Hellweek occurs during this phase. The phase also accounts for most of the DORs or dropouts.

2nd Phase of BUDS – This phase, called *Dive Phase*, is 2 months long and predominantly focuses on the basics of *Combat Swimmer* training. The legendary training evolution known as *Pool Comp* occurs during the third week of this block of training.

3ʳᵈ Phase of BUDS – This phase, known as the *Land Warfare* phase of training, focuses on the basic operational training tactics employed during any land operation. This is the final phase of BUDS that finishes with a four week *hammer session* on *The Rock*.

5 Paragraph Op Order – A military planning strategy used primarily in small unit tactics. The 5 paragraph Op order breaks the mission down in 5 distinct stages of planning, ensuring units don't miss critical facets of any operation. Traditionally they include the Situation, the Mission, the Execution, Administration and Logistics and Command and Control.

Actionable Intelligence – After receiving or gathering enough important information, you decide that the information is worthy of being called intelligence. The *Intel* is then applied to your life in a way that enhances your ability to achieve *mission success*.

Animaintel – The soulful intelligence one learns from others by allowing the intellectual breath of life to inflate one's soul with an infinite desire to physically, mentally and spiritually live a Team Life to its fullest.

Bear Crawl – The physical act of placing your hands on the ground along with your feet and moving from one place to another. This is usually reserved for a student in BUDS as a form of punishment.

Big Goals – The Life Missions you establish in order to achieve your dreams.

Boat Crew – In BUDS, students are assigned to working groups of 6 or 7 men. Many evolutions in training are designed to test and enhance a student's commitment to living the Team Life by hammering their Boat Crews. Examples include *Surf Passage*, *Rock Portage* and *Log PT*.

Boots on the Ground – A term used to describe how a person's actions are directly representative of their statements.

Breakout – This is the first hours of Hellweek when instructors unleash a furious hammer session on the students. Many students quit during this evolution.

Bring the hate - This is a common phrase in the military. It relates to giving the enemy a dose of lead, bombs or any other fatal ordinance. It also can be used as a description to describe a self-induced *hammer session*.

Brown Shirts – When students complete Hellweek they are instructed to wear brown t-shirts, designating them as further along in training.

BUDS – Basic Underwater Demolition SEAL School. A 24-week intensive special operations training program. Many consider BUDS to be the most difficult training program in the world.

Chow Hall – A Navy Dining facility.

Chucklehead – A Knucklehead who thinks he's funny.

Cold, Wet and Sandy – The primary physical state that BUDS students feel as they go through training.

Combat Nap – A brief snooze taken by a soldier during a momentary pause in fighting or training.

Comfort Zone – The physical, mental and spiritual space in a person's mind that protects them from possible failure or fear.

Comfort Zone Behavior – Learned emotional and cognitive behavior human beings use to create the physical, mental and spiritual boundaries in their life that protect and mitigate from feeling and thinking about logical or illogical fear.

DECON Shower – A set of decontamination spray pipes positioned just outside of the *Combat Training Tank* on the Naval Amphibious Base in Coronado, California. BUDS students are ordered to rinse off beneath these freezing cold pipes prior to entering the *CTT*.

Demo Pit – A training area used in BUDS to hammer students. The final evolution of Hellweek takes place in the Demo Pit when students are forced to low crawl, traverse high ropes and sit in filthy water for extended periods of time. After being awake for 5 days this seems like an eternity.

Direct Action – A type of mission in special operations that usually delivers a higher-level violence of action against an enemy force. A focused regimented approach to achieving a specific task in your daily life.

Dirty Name – An obstacle on the BUDS O' Course that hammers people.

Dive Pair – A pair of students who are responsible for each other's safety, performance and all around behavior during any evolution involving diving.

DOR – Drop on Request. Any time a student wants to quit the SEAL program, due to his voluntary status, he simply requests to be dropped from training.

Drop – An order given by an instructor to a student requiring the student to perform 20 perfect pushups.

Drop Dead date or time – This is an absolute time. This time is not flexible because of your procrastination or excuses.

ENDEX – End of Exercise. When a military training evolution has reached its conclusion it is considered to be ENDEX.

Effective Fire – Effective fire refers to a shooter's ability to put their rounds accurately on target.

Evolution – An evolution is any military or life training event or experience that has a specific beginning and ending. Hellweek is an uber evolution in BUDS. Getting married is an uber evolution in Life.

Flash Bang – A small explosive device used in assault operations to disorientate the enemy. The small handheld explosive device is thrown into a room prior to entrance.

Fight or Flight Response – a theory made popular by Walter B. Cannon suggesting that all animals have a primal, sympathetic nervous response to external stimulus that enables them to fight or flee in an adverse situation.

Fire Team – In a SEAL Platoon, four men make up a fire team. In life your fire team is your closest swim buddies, the humans who can get you out of trouble when you need them.

Fire in the Gut – A SEAL motto that describes the insatiable desire to be better, to push yourself harder and to achieve mission success no matter what the cost.

Fragged – When a solider is hit with a piece of debris from a bullet or projectile. When a human being is hit with a piece of negativity.

Free Surface Ascent – This is a dive term that relates to a diver moving from depth to the surface in a slow gradual manner, exhaling the entire way to the surface so they don't suffer an embolism.

Forging – The process of shaping metal by using compressive forces coupled with intense heat. The process of shaping your *Self-Confidence* by using 8 Froglogic Life Missions.

Froglogic Negativity Grid/ FNG – A simple chart rating system to decide what is negative in your life.

Froglogic Mission Planning Outline – An outline designed to help you establish a functional process of setting goals in your life.

Frogman – A Frogman is a term originally used during WWII to describe the Underwater Demolition Team members of the Navy. A term now used to describe Navy SEALs.

Front Sight Focus – An instructional term used in Combat Pistol and Rifle training. The term refers to the shooter's need to focus their vision solely on the front sight of the pistol or rifle just prior to squeezing the trigger. A Froglogic term referring to a person's need to stay focused on the main purpose behind any action.

Full Benefit – In BUDS when students decide to improvise or alter orders   the slightest bit, instructors often reward them with an extra hammer session, thereby giving them full benefit.

G2 – In the Army, an officer in charge of intelligence is considered the G-2 in the chain of command. This can also be used to describe any critical information that will help or impede your ability to achieve mission success.

Gig Line – A military term used to describe the aligned stitching running down the front of a soldier's uniform.

Get By – Getting by on someone is a form of beating the system in an unfair manner.

Get Squared Away – A never-ending commitment towards doing the little things in your life that ultimately lead to an emotional stability and cognitive focus.

Getting Hammered – Taking a physical or mental beating in relation to life's experiences.

Goon Squad – A group of students who can't physically or mentally meet the standards of a particular evolution. This group is then physically and mentally remediated during and after the evolution in order to motivate them never to end up in the Goon Squad again.

Hammer Session – A well thought out and planned beating designed to inflict just enough physical and/or mental pain to alter one's perception of their world around them.

Hellweek – A 5 day ultra-evolution in BUDS that acts as the initial gateway for young tadpoles who want to become SEALs. This is the first real physical, mental and spiritual test a young recruit faces in their career. See glossary for evolution definitions.

High Order – When an explosive charge completely detonates, having the desired effect with the intended application. When an instructor loses his mind with frustration or gains focus with tortuous intent and delivers a massive hammering.

High Speed – Performing the basics to perfection.

Human Being – A person who possesses and uses empathetic logic and focused behavior to guide life's journey.

I Got Mine – An attitude based on narcissism that breaks down the *Team Life* spirit.

Indian Runs – A group of people running in a single file formation where the last runner sprints to the front of the line as the rest of the runners jog.

Kill the man with the ball – A childhood game I played with two or more players. One player picks up the football and evades tacklers as long as possible. Once the runner is tackled to the ground the ball is tossed randomly into the air for another person to catch and begin evading tacklers.

Kit Up – When SEALs or other SOF units get ready to commence clandestine operations, they put on the specific equipment needed to conduct the mission.

Knock Out – Finishing something with speed, focus and diligence.

Knucklehead – A person acting like an idiot.

Letterman Complex – A person who psychologically attributes his current physical and mental fortitude to his past accomplishments.

Life's Gear Bag – The critical cognitive and emotional memories, thoughts and lessons learned that you keep stored in your mind. This gear is essential for completing all missions in your life. Take care of your gear and your gear will take care of you.

Life Instructor – A strong, knowledgeable figure in your life that instructs you how to achieve *mission success* in the face of extreme adversity.

Life Ops – The Small Goals of your daily life that shape your ability to succeed.

Life Missions – A person's purpose or objective that is driven by the perpetual desire to develop his or her physical, mental and spiritual self for the greater good. The Big Goals in your life.

Mission Critical – The critical aspects of an operation. The necessary focus required to achieve your dreams.

Mission Success – The comprehensive success you feel physically, mentally and spiritually after achieving a Life Mission.

Motivational Triggers - Anything that makes you feel awesome about where you are in life and grateful for just being alive.

Neuromuscles – The mental muscles of your mind needed to forge your *Self-Confidence*.

O Dark Thirty – Really early in the morning. Before the sun rises.

OJT – On the Job Trauma – The psychological trauma received when you are subjected to constant belligerence because of unsatisfactory training from your bosses, managers and supervisors.

Pass the Monkey – When a person pushes the responsibility for his or her life onto the back of someone else.

Pay the man – When a BUDS class or student pays the instructor staff for failure to follow orders or poor behavior. Usually involves a hammer session.

Phase Lines – The different timelines of an operation. Primarily used in Mission Planning.

Ping – When an instructor singles you out and repeatedly hammers you.

Platoon – In the SEAL Teams, a platoon consists of 16 men. Each man in the platoon has a specific job description and operational assignment. However, all SEALs are cross trained to be able to perform each other's job in an emergency.

PMA – Positive Mental Attitude – A psychological state of mind that fortifies your ability to physically, mentally and spiritually resist negativity.

PT Disorder – A psychological disorder that inhibits you from physically taking care of your body and living a healthy lifestyle.

PTRR – This was a pre-training or transitory phase during my time in BUDS.

Real Time – This is a factual experience happening right now in your life.

Respect – The positive emotional and cognitive recognition of yourself, another person or entity based on the specific or intended actions of those parties.

Ring Out – When a BUDS student decides that SEAL training isn't for them, they DOR and then ring the BUDS bell to confirm their decision.

UNSAT – Unsatisfactory

SA – Situational Awareness - The comprehensive ability to collect, assess, dismiss and act upon *real time* emotional and cognitive data resulting from the constantly changing external and internal environments that govern your physical, mental and spiritual experiences.

Silver Strand – The strip of land running from Coronado to Imperial Beach. A thin slice of beach where lots of SEAL training takes place.

Small Goals – Daily Ops or tasks that need to be achieved in order to create good habits in a person's life.

Sniping – The act of taking a long range shot with a precision weapon. The act of targeting something significant in your life you want to take control of.

Suck Factor – A rating system for your physical, mental and spiritual status. For instance, when you have been getting *hammered* for 72 hours straight, the *Suck Factor* is high.

Sugar Cookie – When students are ordered to cover their bodies head to toe with sand. Having it in every orifice of your body and your uniform saturated with the fine particulate makes conducting any evolution feel like you're wearing sandpaper.

Surf Hit – During Pool Comp, students are pushed to their limits by instructors as they suffer through four different stages of simulated *Surf Hits*. Instructors do everything to disorient the students, including turning off their air and inflicting serious problems upon the students' breathing loops.

Surf Torture – A disciplinary act used in BUDS to train students in a variety of psychological topics. Students are ordered to lock arms and as a class walk into the chilly waters of the Pacific Ocean. Once they reach a particular depth, they lie on their backs and spend an appropriate amount of time thinking about how to improve as a class.

Surf Zone – The area of water in the ocean ranging from the outside break to the crest of the daily tide. An area used to train students in a multitude of evolutions, the most notable being *Surf Torture*.

The Jericho Mile – The toughest but most rewarding

portion or distance traveled during any Life Mission or personal storm.

The Bell – A large nautical bell positioned outside of the 1st Phase office. When a student decides to quit training, their request is reviewed by the phase officer and then granted once the student is sure of his decision. The student then rings the bell three times to signify his final decision to quit.

The Pit – An area in BUDS where student gear cages are located. A place where students are allowed to congregate with some protection from the wrath of the instructors.

The SEAL Zone – An intuitive, Zen like state when SEALs reach an operational capacity that magnifies their ability as a team to crush their opponents. This state of mind is the result of thousands of hours forging their *Self-Confidence* and living the *Team Life*.

Twin 80's – In BUDS, while going through the initial part of Dive Phase, students use two aluminum or steel air cylinders for dive operations.

Verbal Flash Bangs – A short, explosive comment used to stun your opponent when you're engaged in a verbal jujitsu.

Verbal Jujitsu – The art of tying your opponent in knots by using their own illogical commentary against them.

Wammy Knot – The final stage of Pool Comp, when the instructor creates an unsolvable problem in the diver's breathing loop and forces the student to surface after attempting to get the knot untied.

Warning Order – A crisis mission planning order that calls you into action. A direct order to change your life, given by a teammate.

Warrior Poet - A human being balanced by his or her reluctant willingness to fight for and defend the moral truth while joyously sucking the marrow out of everything life has to offer.

Whining – The infectious negativity spewed out of someone's mouth when they have lost the intestinal fortitude to endure life's challenges.

White Shirts – When students first enter BUDS, part of their initial gear issue is a white shirt. This signifies they have yet to finish *Hellweek*.

BUDS EVOLUTIONS:

4 Mile Timed Run – A testable and timed evolution that students are required to pass on a weekly basis. The run takes place along the shoreline, regardless of tide and surf conditions. Students will battle with extremely soft, sluggish sand or wide, flat, hard packed conditions. With each new phase

the time requirements are shortened to increase pressure on the students. This evolution may occur multiple times in one week.

2 Mile Ocean Swim – A testable and timed evolution that students are required to pass on a weekly basis. The swim takes place just outside of the farthest surf break, no matter what the water conditions are like. Students will battle with heavy currents, frigid water and choppy water. With each new phase the time requirements are shortened to increase pressure on the students. This evolution may occur multiple times in one week.

O' Course – The Obstacle Course is a testable and timed evolution that students are required to pass on a weekly basis. The O' Course is one of the toughest in all of the military. Students battle constant fatigue and many times get hammered prior to beginning the course. With each new phase the time requirements are shortened to increase pressure on the students. This evolution may occur multiple times in one week.

Hellweek - A 5 day ultra-evolution in BUDS that acts as the initial gateway for young tadpoles who want to become SEALs. This is the first real physical, mental and spiritual test a young recruit faces in their career. See glossary for evolution definitions.

Pool Week - A 5 day ultra-evolution in BUDS that acts as the secondary gateway for young tadpoles who want to become SEALs. This ultra-evolution involves a series of testable evolutions that include Buddy Breathing, Ditch and Don, Night Ditch and Don, Buddy Ditch and Don and Pool Comp.

Pool Comp - A major testable evolution in 2nd Phase. This massive hurdle for students occurs at the end of Pool Week. This evolution tests a student's comfort level in the water under extreme stress. The instructors inflict four different types of problems upon the student's breathing loop, including the Wammy Knot.

Surf Passage – This is an evolution designed and implemented to test a Boat Crew's ability to work together in extreme conditions. Students battle with giant surf, cold water and extreme exhaustion.

Soft Sand Conditioning Runs – This evolution is a hard-core gut check. A class is mustered on the beach as they prepare to be led at a blistering pace through the soft sand. Instructors are known to use every possible inch of the Silver Strand in order to pulverize students. If students fail to keep up with the lead instructor and the main pack, they are separated during the run and hammered extensively. This is called the Goon Squad.

Steel Pier – This evolution usually happens on the second night of Hellweek. Students are patrolled to a section of piers on NAB. The students are then ordered into San Diego Bay where they are expected to tread water, disrobe and perform personal lifesaving techniques. After an extended period in the water, the students are instructed to exit the water with all their clothing and lay flat, bare back against the pier for an undetermined period of time.

Around the World – This evolution takes place on Thursday night of Hellweek. Boat Crews are ordered to paddle from the BUDS *Surf Zone* around Coronado Island and back to the opposite side of the Silver Strand from BUDS. This evolution takes place when students have had less than one hour of sleep in four days and can last up to 14 hours.

Drown Proofing – Considered one of the most challenging testable evolutions in BUDS, Drown Proofing occurs in 1st Phase and tests a student's comfort level in the water. The student's hands are tied behind his back at the wrist and his feet are tied together at the ankle. Students are then ordered into the 9' section of the CTT. Students are required to bob off the pool floor for 10 minutes. Next, students are required to float in the same spot for 5 minutes. Then they are required to swim 200 meters back and forth across the pool. Finally students must bob for another 10 minutes, grab a mask off the pool bottom with their teeth and conduct a forward and backward flip, and finish with 5 minutes of bobbing with the mask still in their mouth. This evolution was created because of the miraculous escape made by a Navy SEAL during Vietnam and is designed to simulate his unbelievable effort escaping his captors down a river with his hands and feet tied.

50 meter Underwater Swim – This testable evolution challenges students to push past their self-induced fear of drowning. A student is ordered to jump feet first into the pool, conduct a forward flip and begin traveling underwater, across the pool, touch the other side and return taking only one breath.

Underwater Knot Tying – Another extremely difficult testable evolution that happens during 1st Phase. Students are positioned in the 3' section of the CTT. Instructors are stationed in the 15' section of the pool treading water above a trunk line positioned to grommets on the bottom of the pool. Students are ordered to wade out to the 9' section and tread water while they wait to be called into the 15' section. When the instructor is ready, he summons the student to wade closer and position himself above the trunk line. The instructor then orders the student to swim down to the trunk line and tie one or more of the five testable knots onto the trunk line. The student must swim down, tie his small piece of rope onto the trunk line using the proper knot, give an okay, have it inspected by the instructor, receive an okay back, untie the knot and return to the surface. If the student ties all knots correctly, he passes the evolution.

Log PT – This evolution tests a Boat Crew's ability

to work together while they get *hammered* with a 200 lb., 8' telephone pole. Boat Crews are instructed to perform rigorous exercises and races on the beach while they maintain positive control of the heavy pole. Students battle extreme fatigue and complete exhaustion during this crusher.

Grinder PT – This evolution is very similar to the PT routines I posted at the beginning of each mission, except it lasts much longer, has many more reps and usually ends in the student being wet, cold and sandy. This evolution is a great opportunity for instructors to single out students and *hammer* the snot out of them.

SEAL MOTTOS

"The only easy day was yesterday"
"Easy Day"
"Never Quit"
"Never leave a man behind"
"Attention to Detail"
"Pays to be a winner"
"Plan your dive, dive your plan"
"One is none"
"Take care of your gear and your gear
will take care of you"
"You are only as fast as your
slowest guy"
"Smooth is fast"
"You know the deal"
"No Pain, no gain"
"HOOYAH"

Acknowledgments

I want to thank all those in my life who loved, taught and hammered me. I also want to apologize to all those who had to deal with me when I lacked the Self-Confidence I have now. Thank you for teaching me how to fail. To all those I am helping now, and plan on helping in the future, standby, it's my mission to help you achieve your dreams. HOOYAH!

To my wife, you are the reason I have become what I am now. Thank you and I love you.

To my parents, thank you for forging my foundation. I love you.

To my editor, mentor and father, Charlie Rutherford, thank you. The gifts you have given me are a blessing. I am the luckiest son in the world.

Editor's Note

Working with David to edit "SELF CONFIDENCE," the first FIELD MANUAL FOR ADULTS published by FROGLOGIC CONCEPTS LLC Leadline Publishing Division, has been a collaborative effort to bring readers David's unique vision of how to live a better, healthier more productive and happy life. Learning from David's extraordinary personal life experiences which forged the man he is today can and will benefit every reader. Each of us goes through life forming and operating within teams, from our initial nuclear family team, our extended family teams, our school teams, our work and community teams and our life career teams. The success of our team life in each instance depends upon our commitment, dedication, discipline and self-assurance.

David's many successful team commitments ultimately were tested to the core. From this period of lost self-confidence, David committed to returning himself to the high performance team member he had always been by electing to join the Navy and become a Navy SEAL. Taken from his years as a SEAL Team member and Instructor, David incorporates those same principles of uncompromising hard work, total commitment and absolute discipline into his Froglogic Concepts lifestyle programs and philosophy to aid the reader in making life changing decisions as to lifestyle and life challenges.

In a time of explosive worldwide communication access and learning opportunity never before available, we are, ironically, experiencing a crisis in shared community values, factionalism, loss of positive dialog and hyper-negative thinking with resultant sensory degradation. These negatives have come to dominate large portions of every day life for each of us in business and in our personal lives. The result is that it takes ever more courage to live a life committed to positive thinking, sustaining our core values and disciplined team commitment. David and Froglogic bring a philosophy to counter cultural negativity by substituting positive step-programs to enhance the disciplined self and broaden team life by both sharing his invaluable, poignant hard lessons learned and by translating those lessons into the broadest application for everyone.

David's courage, humility, vision and unwavering commitment to helping others of all ages, communities and backgrounds forge and achieve their personal life goals is inspirational and a proven method for success. Our nation is justifiably proud of our selfless military personnel and the meritocracy of our military branches which promote an honorable life of selfless commitment, service and duty, putting the greater good before personal pleasures and self interests, while creating many noble citizen-solders like David and his SEAL Team Brothers. Embodying the best American and historical cultural values, that Team message is as timeless today as ever, and perhaps even more so.

In reading "SELF CONFIDENCE," David asks you to reflect on your own ongoing journey toward your chosen personal changes happening in your heart, mind and spirit as you embrace the FROGLOGIC philosophy, thereby jump-starting your journey to obtain your highest personal success and team success. While "SELF CONFIDENCE" is first about you individually, you will quickly come to understand that David's Froglogic philosophy progresses from self to teams to community, incorporating the Froglogic Missions into your life journey, thereby supporting the life-sustaining and uplifting good life model set forth in "SELF CONFIDENCE."

Congratulations on becoming a Team Froglogic member! Now lace up those boots, or cross-trainers, and prepare for your new and exciting life of positive challenges and personal success you'll find through living the FROGLOGIC LIFE!

Charlie Rutherford
Editor/Team Member

For more information about Navy
SEAL, Motivational Speaker, Author and
Life Instructor

David Rutherford

Please visit

www.teamfroglogic.com

FROGLOGIC
FIELD MANUALS FOR ADULTS

Self-Confidence

by

David Rutherford

Navy SEAL